INTRODUCTION

Minecraft is a worldwide phenomenon. Since it was first released back in 2011, it's been taken to the hearts of thousands and thousands of gamers. And if they're anything like us, they spend hour after hour exploring its many possibilities. Whether you play Minecraft on a tablet, on a desktop computer or on a games console, infinite fun is what you're going to get.

Minecraft, though, is also a game of secrets. It's a game where clever strategies, lateral thinking and some expert help can really unlock even more possibilities. That's where this guide comes in. Whether you're a new Minecraft player or a very experienced one, we've got lots of things to tell you about that we've uncovered while playing the game.

We've packed this book with as many secrets, pieces of advice, tactics and ideas as we can. So whether you want to get on top of the basics of effective building, pillage a Jungle Temple or take down the Ender Dragon himself, we've got plenty to tell you about. Without further ado...

CONTENTS

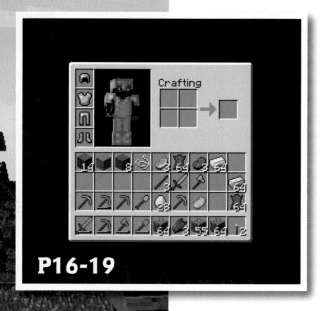

P16-19

P32-33

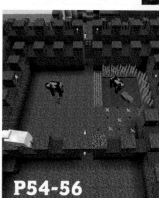

P54-56

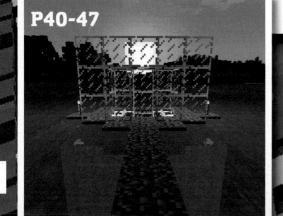

P40-47

P96

P101-106

P132-135

P117-119

SIMPLE TIPS TO GET YOU GOING

S o let's get down to work. Before we go into the depths of *Minecraft* later on in this book, we need to get some of the basics right. Therefore, whether you're a complete beginner or just after a refresher of the foundations of playing *Minecraft*, this is the chapter for you. Here, we're going to take you through your first steps playing *Minecraft*, and helping you familiarise yourself with it. Then, we're going to go through the all-important skill of crafting. We're also going to look at a couple of other things that you'll need to be on top of in order to succeed at *Minecraft*: your first mine, and biomes.

Once we've done all of that, we're rounding this chapter off with a collection of essential tips that should see you up and running in the game in no time. All in all, when you get to the end of page 29, you should have what you need to fully begin your *Minecraft* adventure!

FIRST STEPS
IN A NEW WORLD

You're at your most vulnerable when you first step into a new Minecraft world. Here are some beginner's tips to survive...

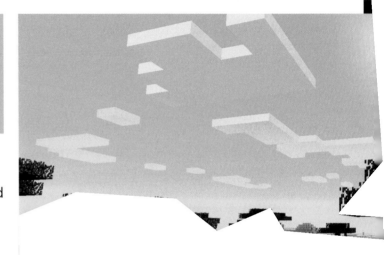

Get wood!

So, you've been dropped into a brand new world with little to your name but the shirt on your back. You can hear animals all around you, and see an endless landscape stretching out into the distance. There's a world of possibilities, but if you're going to see them, you'll need to get moving, and the very first thing you need to do is get some wood.

Before night falls, which takes around 10 minutes of game time, you'll need to do a couple of things, and one of those is to get wood so you can make rudimentary tools, including the all-important crafting table. This is used to make other tools and items, so as soon as you arrive in a new game, find a tree and start punching. You'll need four blocks of wooden planks to create a crafting table, and each block of wood you cut down makes, as luck would have it, four wooden plank blocks.

When chopping down trees, you'll often pick up saplings. If you're in an area where you're going to be living, it's a good idea to plant these saplings, as it'll ensure that you've always got enough trees to harvest for wood.

With a crafting table in hand, you can make some basic wooden tools if you like, chief of which should be a pickaxe. You can also make an axe, spade and, for defence, a sword, but this isn't really necessary, as we'll soon have a better option, so it's a good idea to save your wood.

If you start a game and you're not in a forest or jungle, stood in the middle of a desert, for example, then you'll need to move and find trees ASAP. If you can see greenery in the distance, head towards it right away. If all you can see is sand, you're just going to have to pick a direction and start moving!

Stony ground

Before we get to the proper crafting you'll need the other most useful basic material, and that's cobblestone. To get this easily, use your hands to dig down into the ground until you hit stone, then use the wooden pickaxe to gather some cobblestone.

When digging in *Minecraft*, it's often not a good idea to dig right down, as you don't know what or, more importantly, what isn't below you. Always dig diagonally, making stairs downwards. The same can be said for digging upwards too.

Craft your basics

Now that you've got plenty of wood and stone, with these you can create the basic stone tools – a pickaxe, axe, shovel and sword. Now you can mine all of the basic building blocks, from dirt and stone, to iron and coal, and you can build yourself a simple home to seek shelter in when the nasties come out. Your sword will also let you hunt animals for food, which is essential. You should also build a furnace out of eight block of cobblestone too, as this is another essential item.

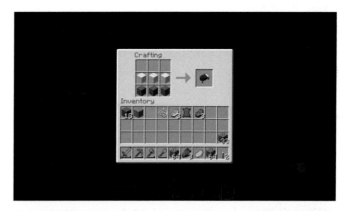

With stone tools, your job is much easier

As soon as you find some cobblestone and you've built a furnace, upgrade to stone tools as soon as you can if you decided to make wooden ones, they're far more useful, and just as easy to craft.

Making fire

Before it gets dark you'll want to make sure you have some light, otherwise you'll be stuck in the dark listening to spiders squeak and zombies moan from places unknown. Basic lights are fashioned out of sticks and either coal or charcoal (made by burning wood, such as wood blocks), and are without a doubt one of the most essential items to carry at all times, especially if you plan on mining or exploring caves, which we'll get to later.

Light sources are also indispensable around the home (see next tip), as they not only let you see, but keep away many monsters. Most mobs in *Minecraft* won't spawn in bright light, so if you blanket your home with light, you'll be all the more protected, even without walls and other traditional barriers.

Torches are one of the most important items in the game, always have plenty on you

Your first 'house' will usually be a simple, mocked up shelter, like this one

Stone Pickaxe

Shelter

You'll quickly want to make sure you've got a safe place to hide overnight, so your next step should be to throw up a basic shelter. It doesn't need to be anything special at this stage, just four walls and a door. You can build out of anything, even dirt, so if you don't have decent materials, just make do.

Many beginner *Minecraft* players make the mistake of trying to build an elaborate house right away, and this is often a mistake. In your first day you simply don't have the time to get creative, so a basic shelter is by far the best option. You can spend more time sculpting the perfect home when you have more time and resources. Of course, part of the battle is picking a good spot for your home. It's easier to hollow out a cliff wall than build a structure from scratch, but if you're in the middle of a desert or flatland, this isn't an option. Building a structure with clear lines of visibility means you can clearly see any threats.

You may spawn near an NPC village, which you may think is a good thing, but it's not. Although there are ready built houses and villagers to trade with, these houses are probably occupied, and you'll only be able to trade with villagers when you have emeralds, which you'll not get for a while. More importantly, at night time the zombies attack, making the whole area very dangerous. If you get a bed made on your first day, you could sleep through the night, thereby stopping zombies from spawning, but it's not a good idea to build too close to such villages.

A door makes it easier to get in and out of your shelter, and you can see out of it. You can build one with six wooden plank blocks and place it in an open space for a doorway. If you don't have the wood, and night is closing in, simply block yourself in until morning. It's worth noting that zombies can break through wooden doors on hard difficulty, so be vigilant if you hear their characteristic moaning.

You'd better get a sword and go hunting, or you'll start to get hungry quick

A good tip to remember is that you can quickly throw up a tiny room-like shelter anywhere in the world at any time. So, if you're stuck out and about exploring and night comes, leaving you no time to get home, simply build a small room and sit inside it until morning. You can even dig a hole in the ground, get in it and cover the hole in a pinch.

Regardless of your chosen type of shelter, always flood it with light, inside and out, this will prevent monsters from spawning. This isn't a problem for smaller houses and hidey holes, but larger buildings can easily spawn mobs if there's not enough light.

A brightly lit home also has another benefit – you can see it from far away, which is useful if you're lost and can't find your way back home to bed. It's also a good idea, especially early on, to build high columns and put lights on top. These act as guideposts that you can see from a distance. In a pinch, you can even build a column and stay on top of it for the night. To make one, you need to master block jumping.

To do this, simply look down, jump and then quickly place a block. Repeat the process until your column is high enough. To get down, either dig your way back down, or build your way down slowly, placing blocks as steps.

Hunt!

With basic tools in hand, you'll need to head out and find food, otherwise you'll start to get hungry. If your hunger meter isn't full, your health won't regenerate, and you'll not be able to perform some actions, such as sprinting (if the hunger bar drops below 3 drumsticks). If you're playing on Hard, and the bar drops all the way, you're health will start to drop and you'll eventually die if you don't eat anything. On Normal difficulty your health won't drop below half of a heart, and on Easy hunger won't lower your heath below five hearts.

So, to keep yourself in good form you'll need to eat, and the best food this early on is, sorry vegetarians, animals. Cows and pigs in particular are the best source of food as they're easier to catch. Chickens are good too, and can also drop feathers, but you'll only get one chicken per kill, whereas cows and pigs can drop more food each. Cooked pork chops are one of the best foodstuffs in the game, filling four drumsticks (raw restores only two).

To cook your food, the best way is to use a furnace, which is made out of eight cobblestone blocks. You'll need to fuel too, such as wood (or wooden items), coal or charcoal. With fuel in place, shove in the food and you'll be cooking a tasty meal in no time. Cooked meat is always better than raw. Raw doesn't only heal you less, but can also poison you, which will drain health.

Gather supplies

Once you've gotten some of the basics – some tools, a shelter and some food, it's time to begin the hard slog of gathering resources to further your adventure. We're going to cover all of this in much more detail later on, but to begin with you'll need to prepare, and this means storage.

You can only carry so many things on your person, and to store the copious amounts of materials and ore you'll soon be collecting, you'll need chests to store your bounty in.

A basic wooden chest is made using eight wooden planks and can hold 27 stacks of items. If you build two chests and place them together, a large chest will be built. These can hold up to 54 stacks of items.

To help keep tabs on your stores, construct a few chests and use them for different materials. You could have one chest for stone, another for wood, another for food, and so on. This is common sense and makes it far easier to work with large amounts of resources.

Beds are used to skip the night and create new spawn points

Bed time

Although not essential, as you don't actually need to sleep in *Minecraft*, beds serve two major purposes – they skip to the morning when you sleep on them, and once slept in, they serve as your new spawn point should you die. For these two reasons alone, it's well worth getting yourself a bed as soon as you can.

If your new game has started with some sheep nearby, then you're in luck. You'll need to find three wool blocks, along with three wooden plank blocks. Wool is dropped by sheep randomly if killed, and is a guaranteed drop if you use shears. However, at this stage, you'll likely have no iron, so shears won't be an option.

If you can gather the resources, you can craft a bed and place it in your house. Be careful you leave enough room to stand up on top of it though, as when you wake that's what you'll be doing. If there's not enough room to stand, you'll be squashed to death when you wake up, and that's not very nice.

As sleeping in beds skips the night time, it doesn't give some monsters time to spawn, and so your next day should be a little less eventful.

Quick tips

● If you're totally new to *Minecraft*, then it's a good idea to make use of the bonus chest option offered in World Options when starting a new world (not applicable on Hardcore). This chest will spawn close to the player, and contains a few items that'll be of help getting you through your first few nights in the world. Such items as wooden planks, tools and food can be found, and once you've looted it, the chest itself can be mined and picked up. All in all, this is a nice little starter kit.

● It's quite rare, but tree leaves can drop apples when harvested, which can be eaten. If you can't find any animals, this can be one way to find food.

● If you die, you'll drop everything you're carrying, including your tools. When you respawn you have five minutes to return and collect your things before they despawn. If this happens, you've lost them forever, and you'll need to start again. For this reason, in your early days, don't wander too far from your initial spawn point. That way, if you die, you'll be able to get your things back with ease.

● Always build your starting home near your spawn point if you can. This way, just as with your items, you can always easily find your house if you die and respawn.

● Don't make a rookie mistake. Enemy mobs don't

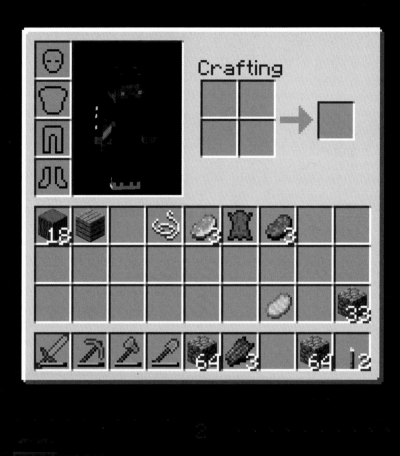

only get spawned at night, they're spawned in darkness. So, even on your first day you can run into creepers and other nasties if you go exploring dark areas. Be warned.

● Chests are for storage, so use them as much as possible. Remember, if you die, you lose what you're carrying, so stowing items in chests can save you a lot of heartache.

● Travel light. It's tempting to carry around masses of food and blocks, but often that's not needed, and you'll run out of space to pick up items and resources. Only take the items you need for a set task. If mining take tools, torches and other supplies. You won't need blocks of stone, as you'll find plenty while you're mining. If you're going fishing, you're not going to need ladders, tons of pickaxes and buckets of water.

● Don't be afraid to take the easy way out if you're having trouble with zombies and other nasties. If you're new to *Minecraft*, just learning the basics of building and mining can be daunting, so enemies can easily tip you over the edge.

  If this is the case, change the difficulty to peaceful. This will give you a far easier time of it as mobs won't be spawned, and you don't need to eat. You even regenerate health automatically if you do take damage.

BASIC

You'll be creating a lot of tools and items in your adventure, but everyone needs to start somewhere

CRAFTING

Inventory crafting

Before you get a crafting table, you'll only have your bare hands with which to craft items. When crafting without a table, you'll only have access to a two-by-two grid, and so your options are limited. This allows the creation of a crafting table, which should always be your first goal in any game, but you can craft other things.

For example, even without a crafting table you can make torches if you have the materials (sticks, coal and/or charcoal). This is important to remember if you're stuck underground without light and no crafting table access.

Durability and speed

The first thing to be aware of when it comes to crafting is material durability and effectiveness, or speed. Each material in *Minecraft* has varying properties, and that also includes the materials you craft tools out of: namely wood, stone, iron, gold and diamond.

Wood is the most basic, and least effective. It's slow and tools break quickly. Stone is better, around twice as durable and fast as wood. Iron is the all-rounder, being twice as durable as stone and around 30% faster at tasks. Gold is an odd one. It's actually weaker when it comes to

durability than wood, but is the fastest material (and great for enchanting). Diamond is the cutting-edge, and always sought after. These tools are around 25 times more durable than wood and very fast.

Ditch the wood

Although it may make perfect sense to create wooden tools, it's actually pretty pointless, as you can mine stone within the first five minutes into a new game. All you really need from a tool point of view is a single wooden pickaxe. This will allow you to mine stone, and once you have that, you can make stone tools, which are far better than wood, so don't waste your time, and save wood for other things. Wooden pickaxes can only mine cobblestone and coal, and will destroy other ores, so you should be careful.

Right tools for the job

Different materials make better tools, but these tools also perform better at their specific task, so this should be noted. For example, although a pickaxe can be used to dig into the ground, it's no more effective than your bare hands. A spade, on the other hand, is far faster. Likewise, a spade will eventually break rock, but a pickaxe is far more suitable. Tools last longer and are far more effective if kept to their roles, so to make your supplies last longer, use them wisely.

Tools used for other purposes will consume more 'uses' per action than normal. For example, a sword hitting a mob with be registered as a single use, whilst a sword breaking a block will use two. The different materials have varying use total per items, as shown here:

WOOD - 60 uses
STONE - 132 uses
IRON - 251 uses
GOLD - 33 uses
DIAMOND - 1,562 uses

An exception to this rule is the hoe. If you hit a mob or break a block with a hoe, it'll register as no uses at all, meaning you'll have an everlasting tool of sorts. Of course, it'll take a long time to do anything (about the same as with your fists), but you'll have all the time in the world.

Pick the axe

Although all of *Minecraft*'s tools are important, you can still feasibly play the game without most of them, ignoring them entirely. Although it'll take a longer time, you can dig without a spade, and you can chop trees without an axe. However, one tool that's truly indispensable is the pickaxe.

Pickaxes are the only tool that can mine precious ores, and some types of pickaxe are needed for specific ores (diamond for obsidian, for example). Other tools simply can't do the job, so your most important tool of all is the pickaxe. It's usually the first tool you'll craft,

and it should always be with you in plentiful supply.

Hoe, hoe, hoe

Hoes are one of the most singularly useful tools in the game, but they're essential for those wishing to utilise farmland and crops. They're used to till the soil so you can plant seeds, and for little else (any tool can farm crops). Bear in mind, however, that hoes till soil at the same pace, regardless of material used, so wood

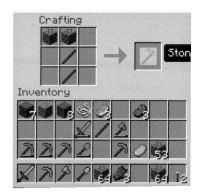

will work the land as fast as diamond. For this reason, don't waste gold or diamond, and stick with stone or iron. Wood is too flimsy, but stone and iron are perfectly durable.

Planking

The first material you'll harvest is wood, and in the world of *Minecraft* it's the most versatile of all resources. It can be used as a building material, tool, weapon, burned and is turned into numerous tools and items. One of the most useful of these is wooden planks. These blocks are one of the most-used to create such things as crafting tables, beds, sticks, chests and much more. So, always ensure you have plenty of trees

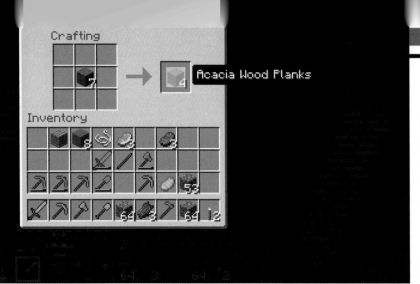

Wooden planks are one of the most useful resources, so always have them in stock

The kinds of armour vary, with the weakest being leather, followed by gold, chain, iron and then diamond as the best armour, but is it really needed?

The best tip for armour is to actually forget about it for the most part. The main overworld can be dangerous, yes, but with practice, and on lower difficulties, it's never really dangerous enough to warrant armour, and losing it all after falling into lava can be infuriating.

(plant saplings), and store plenty of planks. Don't worry about the different wood types, such as spruce, birch and so on, they're all the same, even if they stack separately.

Charred

Early on in the game, when you need light but may not be able to mine coal, you can make use of charcoal to make torches. One of the best ways to do this is to burn wood in a furnace. The Charcoal can then be used with sticks to make torches.

Charcoal also makes for a surprisingly efficient fuel for the furnace. Another efficient fuel type is wooden planks. These burn one-and-a-half items per block, so a wooden log, which makes four plank blocks, can smelt 8 items. Not bad, and certainly useful early on.

Armour?

One of the most resource-heavy items to craft in *Minecraft* is armour. You can craft armour out of leather, iron, gold and diamond, and there's also chain armour. A full suit of armour takes a lot of resources to craft, which isn't so bad for more readily available materials like leather and iron, but gold, and especially diamond, are more valuable.

When venturing to the Nether on the other hand, iron armour is a good idea. Forget leather, gold and diamond. Leather and gold aren't strong enough to be of any use and diamond is far too valuable. There's a good chance you'll lose your armour, as the Nether is a dangerous place, so iron armour is economical enough, and provides enough protection. Chain armour is only obtained by trading with villagers and rare mob drops, so is also a little too valuable to risk.

It's worth noting that leather boots provide roughly same level of protection (half a defence point) as chain and gold boots, so if you want to save that gold, keep the leather, it's more cost effective.

If you're planning on taking on either the Ender Dragon or Wither, however, then spare no expense. Diamond armour is practically a necessity (and enchanted armour at that). By this point in the game, though, you'll likely have been gathering

Make charcoal by burning wood in a furnace if you're low on coal for torches

A suit of diamond armour is great, but you're best saving it for bosses

the repair on top of the two individual tools' remaining uses. This trick is best used if you have two tools that are running very low on durability.

Don't be stingy

When crafting items, don't spare the resources if you have them. You always need numerous tools, and having spares will be a life saver when you're out in the field. For example, if you're going to delve deep into the world and mine some ore, don't simply wander down there with a single pickaxe, craft and take a bunch. Always craft a spare sword, so you're not left defenceless in a tight spot.

resources for some time, and so should have plenty of diamonds to spare.

On a side note, the more aesthetically focused players out there should note that leather armour, whilst the weakest, is the only armour that can be dyed. So, if you want to sport this season's hot colours, this is the armour you'll need.

Two'll fix it

All tools in *Minecraft* have durability ratings, as we've already mentioned, and if this durability runs out your tool will break. However, you don't have to wait for a tool to break, you can combine two of the same type of tool together to repair items.

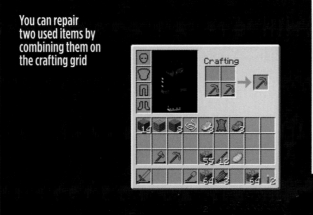

You can repair two used items by combining them on the crafting grid

So, if you've got a couple of used iron pickaxes, you can place them both on the crafting grid and the result will be a repaired iron pickaxe, with the total durability of the two separate tools. The main benefit of this method is that you also get around 5% extra durability out of

Mobile crafting

Don't forget, you can carry a crafting table and furnace with you regardless of what you're doing. It means you can always craft items if you have the resources.

The axeman cometh

If you find yourself in the wild, pursued by foes and you have no sword, you can always use an axe. Although not as effective in combat, they do plenty of damage, and can be a help in a pinch.

YOUR FIRST MINE

The golden rule

To start to mine you have to do one thing, and that's dig. There are few rules in *Minecraft* that have to be stuck to when it comes to playing the game, but one should be obeyed by all, and that's never dig straight down or straight up.

You simply never know what's directly below you in the world of *Minecraft*. It could be more dirt or stone, but it could just as easily be a massive drop into a wide open cave or chasm. Likewise, if you're underground and dig up, you could easily dig right up into water, or even lava.

If you dig straight down, you can easily fall to your doom, and digging straight up may see you covered in lava (not comfy). So, to avoid any such perils, always dig diagonally, making sure you're clear of any drops or nasty surprises.

Staking a cave

You can mine anywhere in *Minecraft*, the entire world can be dug into, smashed up and hollowed out, all the way down to the indestructible bedrock. However, there are better places to start out your mining career, especially if you're just setting out into a world.

The best places for new players and those entering a new world to begin are existing cave structures. They require the least amount of work and tool use, and often yield some great resources. You can easily find bountiful amounts

Caves can be ready-made mines, but are also home to mobs

crafting table and furnace will give you the chance to build anything you need (you'll have wood, and there's stone all over), and the food is self explanatory. With the ability to build anything, you can even throw up a makeshift, underground house to sleep in for really deep mining excursions.

of coal and iron without too much digging, and you may even find a cave with even more valuable ore. However, caves are also mob breeding grounds, so always take a sword.

You should also take a chest or two (or the materials to make them) as you'll likely collect a mass of resources, and you'll soon run out of space, so a base camp with storage is essential.

Be afraid of the dark

Before you even think of going into a cave or digging a mine, you'll need lights, and plenty of them. Never venture below ground without a collection of torches, or at least the means to craft more if you need them.

You'll need these to not only light the way, but also to blanket the tunnels with light to prevent mobs from spawning, ensuring you have a safe and secure mine. Place torches evenly enough to soak the underground pathways with light, and don't be stingy. Dark places can spawn mobs, and the last thing you need when deep underground is to hear that dreaded hissing sound behind you...

Torches also serve as great breadcrumb trails, leading you back out of your mine to the surface. It's very easy to get lost in *Minecraft*.

Dob, dob, dob

As the Scouts would say, always be prepared. You may only think you need a pickaxe or two, some torches and a sword to go mining, but you'd be wrong. You should also take a spare crafting table, furnace, wood and food. The

Iron and stone

Just as a wooden pickaxe cannot be used to mine much more than stone and coal, a stone pickaxe also has limits. Standard (not enchanted) Stone pickaxes can mine stone, coal and iron, but little else. So, if you find precious ores like gold, redstone and diamond, you'll need an iron pickaxe, otherwise you'll destroy the ore as you mine it. So, always have a couple of iron pickaxes to hand, and use the stone pickaxes as your main

Always carry a bucket of water when mining and exploring, it may save your life

digging tools, and only use iron tools when needed.

Obsidian can only be mined using diamond pickaxes, so don't even try with anything else, enchanted or not.

Buckets O' fun

One of the most important items to take with you when mining is a bucket, preferably filled with water. The main reason for this is lava. As you dig deeper you'll often run into pools of lava (but not always, as it can be found closer to ground level too). If this touches you, or you fall in, you'll be set on fire (falling in does much more damage). Once you're on fire, you'll continue to lose heath, and can die in seconds. To prevent an early death if this happens, use a bucket of water to put yourself out.

If you do get set alight by lava and death by burning is inevitable, at least try to get out of the lava and to dry land, as you'll drop all of your items when you die. If this happens and you're still in the lava, all your items will be burned up and destroyed. If you die out of the lava, your items may be fine and you can race back and grab them again.

Blocked off

As you dig, it's a very good idea to have some stone or another solid block ready at a moment's notice. This way, if you accidentally dig into some lava or water when mining, you can quickly plug the hole before the water or lava seeps through. This is harder to do with water, as it runs faster, but usually water won't kill you. Lava will. Luckily, lava flows slowly, so you can usually block it off before any damage is done.

Stop the flow

Often you'll encounter large caves with water or lava falls or even lakes. This can make exploration quite tricky, but you can make things easier. If you can find the source of the flow into the chamber you're in, all you need to do is block it off. Do this correctly, and much of the time, the flow will stop, making it easier for you to wander around and loot the area.

Water ladder

Underground streams and lakes can be a problem a lot of the time, but they can also be a lifesaver. If, for example, you're trapped underground and being pursued by a creeper, you can actually use waterfalls to your benefit by swimming up them out of harm's way. Likewise, if you need to descend a large drop, you can swim down a waterfall safely. If you have a bucket of water, you can create your own waterfalls anywhere, meaning that you've got a one size fits all ladder in your pocket.

Bedrock is indestructible, and marks the bottom of the world

Generally, the Y-11 layer of the world is the most lucrative when it comes to finding rare ore

into lava. Some foes, especially zombies, are pretty dim, and will walk right into lava or water, so use this fact to your advantage.

Suffocation

It's not just water and lava that you have to worry about when it comes to things falling on your head: a couple of other blocks also represent a threat. Sand and gravel are affected by gravity and will fall if nothing is supporting them. If you're caught underneath this, you can suffocate and die. This is another reason why you don't dig straight up.

However, the gravity-obeying properties of these blocks also makes them useful, as they can be used to quickly and easily fill in pools of water and lava, and can be useful when filling in caves or creating stairs downwards.

Defend thyself

It's all too easy to forget that there are other denizens of the world sharing the dark with you, and this can quickly lead to an early grave. Always be vigilant, even when exploring smaller tunnels or caverns. Creepers can pop up from anywhere (even dropping from above), and skeletons can pick you off from a distance, even if you can't see them in the gloom.

As well as using your sword and bow to defend yourself from attack, don't be afraid to use the environment. You can wall off foes with blocks, or even hit them off high cliffs or

Bedrock

No, it's not the Flintstones' home town, it's the very bottom layer of the Minecraft world (and the top and bottom of the Nether). This dark stone emits a dusty particle effect and is totally impervious to damage. Without cheating you can't dig below this and, once you hit bedrock, you can go no further down (if you did you'd end up in 'the void' and die). You may think that this lower level is a goldmine of rare resources, and it can be, but often it's actually better to dig up a few levels, as diamond, for example, is usually found a little higher up than the world's core.

Sweet spot

So, what's the best depth to mine? Due to the random nature of the game, there's no single, spot on answer, but the general rule is to aim for around Y-coordinate of 11 (you can see this in the PC version using the debug display (press F3). Alternatively, you can dig all the way down to bedrock, stand on the topmost bedrock block and dig six blocks upwards. Lava pools often also form at around this depth. The Y-11 level contains every type of ore, so the odds of hitting some are higher, including diamond and gold.

A FORAGER'S GUIDE TO BIOMES

Part of the joy of *Minecraft* is the thrill of exploration and the tingle you feel upon finding something new. Who can ever forget finding their first vein of diamonds? Or the first time they looked directly at an Enderman?

This doesn't just apply to what you can find deep underground whilst mining, or to the creatures you might encounter. It also applies to the different biomes you'll encounter, and, believe us, there are plenty of surprises out there.

Minecraft today features around 70 biomes, some of which are slight variants on others but many of which are unique. Many less common blocks and resources can only be found in specific biomes, so we're here to explain what you can find in *Minecraft*'s various biomes.

1 Snowy Biomes

Starting a new game and finding yourself in a Snowy biome can be a tough prospect. In the early game the fight for survival is challenging thanks to Snowy biomes' few, scattered trees and their sparse neutral animals, meaning light and food are hard to come by. This is not what you want as you prepare to survive your first few nights. Fortunately snowy biomes are potential sources of some uncommon resources – plus a couple that are entirely unique – which can work out well further down the line!

The rarest by far is packed ice, which you'll only find in the Ice Plains Spikes biome. You'll know when you've found one when you spot its unmistakable ice spikes reaching up into the sky. These spires are made up of packed ice, which is far superior to regular ice for construction purposes. Why? Well, light sources don't melt it, for a start! They're also not transparent, meaning you'll have a little privacy in your ice fortress. The downside is that these ice spikes are very rare.

Aside from packed ice you'll not be surprised to find no shortage of snow in these biomes, which is handy for igloos or weirder creations like snow golems. You'll also come across wolves, spruce trees and the

Snow biomes may be beautiful, but they can also be desolate

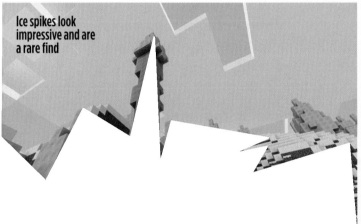

Ice spikes look impressive and are a rare find

Snowy hills hold the promise of rare ores within and beneath

Cold Biomes

2 These biomes may be chilly but at least they're not perpetually coated in a thick layer of snow. You can also find a lot of special resources and blocks in these frigid lands, from decorative moss boulders to the vanishingly rare emerald ore.

It's not all about these uncommon blocks, however: biomes like the Stone Beach are also excellent sources of large quantities of stone, and are safer to mine in the early days of the game when venturing into caverns in search of rare minerals is a much scarier prospect.

Some of the coolest Cold biomes are the Mega Taiga types. These are expansive and flat, a little like the regular densely forested Taiga biomes where wolves and flowers are common, but feature different types of enormous spruce trees. Not only are these an incomparable source of wood and an excellent location for your very own Ewok village (you can take or leave the Ewoks), they also contain a unique type of dirt block called Podzol. Podzol is great for growing mushrooms and other plants, whether or not they're exposed to light.

Mycelium is another block type that's good for this, but Podzol doesn't spread to other block types as Mycelium does, making for much tidier and controllable mushroom farms. Mycelium is also unable to spread to Podzol. No doubt you're already thinking about how you could turn these properties to your advantage...

So about that Emerald Ore: this extraordinarily rare resource type can only be

occasional oak tree, but these can all be found in less harsh biomes.

Our advice is to only stray into snowy biomes if you're out adventuring, are really keen on building something for which you need large quantities of these rare materials, or fancy a spot of ice fishing.

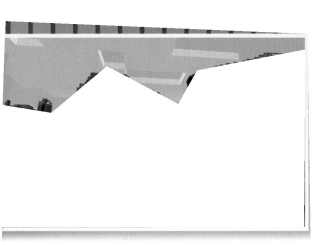

found in the Extreme Hills biome. You may come across mined emeralds elsewhere, but this is the only place to find the ore itself. It will usually appear in single blocks deep underground rather than in veins, and we've usually located it near gold veins.

How do you know when you've found an Extreme Hills biome? Well, there'll be hills about and they'll look pretty extreme! Mountains in these biomes can reach up to about 130 layers (that's just above cloud level), with slopes covered in dull green grass, dirt and stone. They are fairly common – which helps counteract emerald being so rare.

Be warned: Extreme Hills are also the natural habitat of the Silverfish mob. These little critters hide in stone blocks. You won't see them until they attack but you may hear them (a dry, papery, insect-like noise will intermittently be heard when they're hiding nearby). They will sometimes call on all other Silverfish in the vicinity if attacked and swarms can be highly dangerous, so unless you're well-equipped we'd recommend shifting your mining operations elsewhere if you hear that tell-tale Silverfish chitter.

3 Medium/Lush Biomes

Lush biomes are far and away the most commonly encountered; there are also many more variants of Lush biome than any other type. This is no surprise: extensive grasslands, rugged hills, thick forests and beaches have been present in *Minecraft* since before the concept of biomes was introduced, and they're often best for locating the basic resources you need to survive.

What is a surprise is just how many unique treasures are to be found. For starters, the very common Plains biome is the best place to encounter NPC Villages. Villages will only spawn on flat and fairly expansive ground, and Plains are the best such option – although Savanna and Deserts are also possibilities. Plains can also feature horses. They'll appear naturally in small herds of less than six and can be tamed, ridden and bred. When moving at full speed a horse can outrun a minecart, so for players with a lot of ground to cover they're essential – plus you don't have to lay any tracks!

Swampland is also categorised as a Lush biome, though if you ask me they're more like slush. Swamplands are extremely

4 Dry/Warm Biomes

Sand everywhere, and not a drop to drink! You'll never see it raining in these sun-blasted biomes. You will, however, find a plethora of cool resources.

Deserts are the most common Dry biomes, and are great places to locate cacti which can be used as a cheap and effective defence. You can also find

Deserts: the loneliest places in the world

angerous at night thanks to slimes spawning in large numbers. You can also find Witch Huts in Swamp biomes, although at present they don't provide any loot. It's possible that, as Potions continue to be developed and enhanced by Mojang, future versions of the game will feature unique loot in Witch Huts, making Swamplands a lot more interesting.

For now, these soggy biomes are mostly useful as a convenient source of both vines and lily pads, which can be used for a variety of purposes. Vines are a cheap ladder replacement and nice decoration, whilst lily pads allow you to walk on water – perfect for your Jesus impression at *Minecraft* parties.

Roofed Forests are a relatively rare biome that are a bit more exciting than regular forests. The trees you'll find here are so large and dense that their leaves form an almost solid canopy, blocking out a lot of the sun. There's so little light that hostile mobs can spawn here during the day, making them even more dangerous than Swamps. They are, however, the only source of Dark Oak in the game, and huge mushrooms also grow here.

The most exciting Lush biomes are the Jungle biomes. These are among the game's rarest, featuring jungle trees over forty blocks in height and naturally spawning ocelots, cocoa pods, melons and temples.

Ocelots can be tamed into cats, which fend off creepers – the irritating beasts will flee at the sight of a cat. Cocoa beans can be farmed on jungle tree wood and used to produce either cookies or brown dye. Melons can be farmed and – with a slight mod – become Glistening Melons, an important ingredient in brewing potions. But it's Jungle Temples that are the most exciting find: behind puzzles and traps they contain chests full of delicious loot – you could even find emeralds and diamonds in there.

Last is the Mushroom Island biome. As the name suggests these only appear out in the ocean, but they're unique because no hostile mobs spawn in them. That's not to mention the Mooshrooms – cows with mushrooms growing on them – which can be milked with a bowl to get mushroom stew. Okay, that sounds pretty disgusting, but it's also an endlessly renewable food source with no real effort required.

Desert Wells – endless water sources in the barren environment – alongside NPC villages and Desert Temples, which are quite similar to Jungle Temples.

Savannas are also moderately common and are the only natural source of Acacia trees. Acacia wood is the brightest you'll find in *Minecraft*, with a rich orange colour – great for those who want to add a touch of natural vibrancy to their home décor. Otherwise Savannas are only really notable for being another potential location for NPC villages to appear.

Mesas are the rarest and most interesting type of Dry biome, as they're composed almost entirely of clay and red sand. Hardened clay and six kinds of stained clay occur naturally; these seven blocks would otherwise need to be crafted using a furnace and coloured dye. If you're really lucky you may even find the Bryce variant of the Mesa biome, with tall spires of hardened clay rising up from desert below. This is one of the most unique biomes that *Minecraft* has to offer.

More clay than you could ever use, and even better it comes pre-dyed

10 ESSENTIAL TIPS FOR BEGINNERS

1 Get Your Bearings

The spot where you begin your *Minecraft* adventure is called the "spawn point" and you'll reappear there whenever you die. If you're building a base or heading off to explore, make sure you know how to navigate back where you're going from the spawn point. The world of *Minecraft* is infinitely big, so the last thing you want is to end up forced to pick a random direction and walk.

It ain't much to look at, but at least it's finished. And locally-sourced!

A trusty bonus chest marks the spawn point for this new world

2 Start Small

The longest of journeys begins with a single footstep. If you decide that your first creative act in *Minecraft* is to build a scale replica of the Blackpool Tower, you'll soon run into difficulties. Take a while to learn the ropes (and blocks) before embarking on a longer project. It's tempting to aim high when you've seen what can be done, but don't underestimate the satisfaction of completing a small, perfectly-formed project, like a hut or well.

3 Accept Death

As any Zen Master will tell you, accepting your mortality is an important step towards serenity. This is doubly true in *Minecraft*. Even if you

You can't take it with you. But you can run back to where you died and collect it again

You died!

Score: 3

Respawn

Title screen

play on Peaceful mode where enemies are nonexistent, you'll still find ways to die: lava, water, unexpected falls. Don't let it get you down. Death is a part of living, especially in a computer game. Every time you return you'll recover your game quicker and more easily.

4 Use Chests

Just because we don't mind dying, it doesn't mean we like losing stuff. Keeping items in a chest is a great way to help

Cheat death by leaving your spare goodies in a chest for afterwards!

you get back up to speed after you die, and hoarding resources you might otherwise be unable to recover. Chests are simple to build (just eight planks) but can save hours by retaining goods.

5 Know when to hold...

You'll learn quickly enough, but there are three raw materials you should never be without: Wood, Cobblestone and Coal. With those you can make some of the game's most useful items, including furnaces, torches, workbenches, chests, signs and even armour. All the stuff that'll prove invaluable whether you've been playing for five minutes or five months.

6 ...and know when to fold.

Sometimes you'll fill up your inventory and be forced to throw items away, especially if you've been doing a lot of mining. Items with little value include gravel, flint and dirt, all of which are virtually worthless in the quantities you find yourself collecting them. Don't keep too much cobblestone either. Save that space for wood, ores and coal, all of which you can never have too much of!

7 Never Dig Straight Up or Down

You only ever learn this the hard way when you drop into a pool of lava or break a ceiling to find water gushing down on you: never destroy the block you're standing on, or the one directly above you. Smash blocks adjacent to those and if anything goes wrong you should have enough time to correct it before your death becomes a foregone conclusion.

8 Look Out!

If you arrive in a mountainous biome, you can save a huge amount of time by finding coal (and even iron) which is exposed above ground. It's far safer to retrieve surface materials than it is to head underground, so take advantage of it when and where you can.

In the absence of coal, wood burns almost as well

9 Use a Wood-Burning Stove

Coal is essential for fuelling your furnace, but if you've only got a few lumps available, you'll want to save them for making torches – it's virtually impossible to survive without a decent light source, after all. Luckily, you can fuel your furnace in other ways, using wood. Planks, saplings, sticks and even old wooden tools can be placed in the lower slot of a furnace to generate a fire for cooking or smelting.

10 Avoid the Night Terrors

Wandering in the dark might be fun at home, but your house isn't full of monsters that screech and explode when they get too close to you! When playing *Minecraft*, sunset is your reminder to get somewhere well-lit and enclosed. Monsters can't get through doors and walls and sunlight kills them, so use the night hours to do something more sedate, like sleep!

INTERMEDIATE

Now you're up to speed with the basics of *Minecraft*, it's time to start delving into the hidden secrets and strategies that can help you get much, much more out of the game. You don't need us to tell you that there's a lot you need to take into account when playing, and so what we've done in this chapter is go through some of the vital things you need to know in order to make serious progress.

Examples? Well, we're going to look at things such as animal taming, food, farming, building techniques and some more ambitious crafting. We're also going to look at combat and issue some handy tips with regard to picking fights. By the time the chapter comes to a close, we'll have also covered the likes of portals, rare ore and sieges. Once again, we're going to round off with ten more tips to help give you an additional hand when playing our favourite game… *Minecraft*!

TIPS

ANIMAL TAMING

Ocelots become cats when tamed, and can scare away Creepers

Animal aid

Although the majority of the mobs in *Minecraft* are hostile, or serve only as livestock, there are some that can be a lot more beneficial to you, and can be tamed, in turn serving some very useful functions. The tameable mobs currently in *Minecraft* (as of 1.7.4) are the wolf, ocelot and horse. All three can be tamed, but first you'll need to find them.

Wolves are the most plentiful tameable mob in the game, and are found in Forest, Taiga, Mega Taiga, Cold Taiga, and Cold Taiga M biomes.

Wolves are a useful ally, and easily tamed

Saved screenshot as 2013-12-29_13.56.30.png

Ocelots can be tricky to find, and are only found in Jungle biomes. Occasionally they may wander into adjacent biomes, but they only naturally spawn in Jungle areas.

Horses will only spawn naturally in Plains and Savanna biomes, and often spawn in herds. There are three types of horse – horses, donkeys and mules. Each has various breeds (colours). Zombie and skeleton horses can only be obtained with command line cheats.

Wolf taming

The easiest mobs to tame are wolves. All you need to do is find a wolf pack and feed a wild wolf some bones. You have a 1 in 3 chance to tame a wolf with each bone. Once tamed, the wolf will sport a red collar (which can be dyed by using dye on the wolf) and will follow you around. Tamed wolves are often called dogs.

Tamed wolves are around five times stronger than wild wolves, and have around two and a half time the health of a standard wolf. Tamed wolves will attack enemy mobs that attack you, except Creepers.

Using a wolf will toggle its follow or stay state, and you can breed two wolves by feeding them any type of meat (not fish), including chicken, beef or even rotten flesh.

When wolves take damage, they'll show this with their tail, which drops as they get more and more injured. You can heal an injured wolf by feeding it any type of meat.

Be careful you don't attack wolves in the wild as all wolves in range will become hostile, and you could have a fight on your hands.

Ocelot taming

Ocelots are quite tricky to tame, as they're one

of the most skittish mobs in the game initially. You'll need plenty of raw fish and some slight hand movements if you're going to bag one.

Once you find an ocelot in the wild, you need to equip and hold raw fish in your hand. You then need to approach the ocelot very slowly, never looking directly at it. When you're close enough, the ocelot will slowly walk towards you. When it does this, stop moving and don't even turn. When the ocelot gets close and stops, very slowly move your gaze towards it and use the fish. It can take several fish to tame an ocelot, but once you succeed, it'll turn into a cat.

Other factors come into play when taming ocelots. You must have at least a 7x7 area surrounding you, or the ocelot will feel trapped and your taming attempt will fail. Also, there must be no other hostile mobs around, and no other pets.

Once tamed and turned into cats, Ocelots behave similarly to wolves, in that they can be told to follow you or stay. However, unlike wolves, cats don't fight hostile mobs. So, why keep them around? Well, aside from the cute meowing and purring, cats do one very important thing – they scare away Creepers. So, taming a few cats and spreading them around your home is a great way to deter the silent green menace.

You can breed cats by feeding them raw fish.

Horse taming

Taming horses is actually quite simple, but getting the most out of them is more complicated than the wolf or cat. To tame a horse, simply walk up to it and use it with an

empty hand. You'll get onto it and eventually it'll probably throw you off. Keep trying this until hearts appear. This means you've tamed it. You can now place a saddle on the horse, as well as horse armour. Donkeys and mules can also carry chests, for mobile storage.

Horse breeding is a little more complicated than other tameable mobs. To do so you'll need golden apples or golden carrots. The two horses will mate, and produce a baby. This baby will not belong to you automatically, and you'll need to tame it when it becomes an adult after around 20 minutes (feed it golden apples or carrots to speed this growth up). Babies will tend stick with their mothers.

Foals are products of two horses, and will usually have the colour of their parents (but not always). Donkeys can only be bred with two donkeys, and mules are the product of a

Tamed wolves sport collars and can defend you in battle

horse and a donkey. Horses, like other tameable mobs, can be hurt. You can heal them by feeding them apples, bread, golden apples, golden carrots, hay bales, sugar or wheat.

Riding horses

To ride a horse you'll need a saddle (you can ride one without, but it's not controllable). Once equipped, you simply use the horse and control it with the normal directional inputs. You can charge a horse jump by holding jump, and a charge jump can even vault over fences.

Cats scare Creepers, but won't fight mobs

UTILITY MOBS

Snow Golem

It doesn't take much to craft a Snow Golem, and all you need to create one is a couple of snow blocks (made using four snowballs) and a pumpkin. Place two snow blocks, one on top of the other, and then the pumpkin on top. Once you do this, your Snow Golem will spring to life.

Snow Golems aren't the most immediately useful allies as they can't be controlled at all by you, the player (not even told to stay). They wander around on their own leaving a trail of snow behind them, and will attack most hostile mobs, whether they attack you or not. However, they won't attack Creepers or wild wolves (except on the Xbox version, where they can attack Creepers). Mobs they do attack suffer no damage from their snowball projectiles, except Blazes and the Ender Dragon.

Two snow blocks and a pumpkin will create a Snow Golem

Snow Golems aren't the best fighters in the world, but are a good decoy

Using Snow Golems to farm snowballs is easy

Snow Golems are primarily used for defence, but not in an offensive manner much of the time due to their ineffective attack. Instead you should use them as a distraction or at the very least, hindrance. As Snow Golems attack most mobs, they can be useful as a decoy to lead enemy mobs away, and with enough of them on your side, you can use their snowballs to knock back enemies.

Snow Golems can also be very useful for farming snow, as they leave a constant trail of snow cover behind them. Simply build a two block high cage with a single block space in the middle (glass blocks are good so you can see), then build the Golem in the middle and destroy the bottom blocks. The top blocks will trap the golem in place, and you can keep farming the snow trail below the golem, as it regenerates as soon as you mine it. These snowballs can be used to make snow blocks, or as projectiles against enemies weak to snow, such as Blazes.

If you have plenty of fire resistance splash potions, Snow Golems can actually be of great use fighting Blazes in the Nether, as their own snowball attacks damage this fiery foe. This means the Snow Golem is a good ally to use when farming Blaze rods.

Snow Golems can also cause you problems, however. As they're not controllable, they do tend to wander, and can open doors, meaning they can enter your home. This can potentially let enemy mobs in, including Creepers, which could be disastrous.

four iron blocks and a pumpkin will craft a powerful Iron Golem

Keep your Iron Golem on a leash to make sure he doesn't run off

Iron Golem

One the whole, Iron Golems are more useful than the Snow Golem as they're stronger and better in combat. They can take much more damage, and are able to hold their own against almost any threat. They can be found naturally, defending NPC villages, which they are always loyal to, and they can be built by placing four blocks of iron in a T shape, and then placing a pumpkin on the top. Once done, the Iron Golem will spawn.

As with Snow Golems, Iron Golems cannot be directly controlled, and they'll exercise their own will. In fact, unlike Snow Golems, which are loyal to you, Iron Golems are loyal only to villagers, even if you've created them. If not contained in your home, they'll wander off. They only place they'll stay put willingly is a village. You can use a lead on a Golem, and this will keep it in check.

Iron Golems are very slow, and they'll only attack enemy mobs within five blocks unless they're defending a village, in which case they'll hunt all nearby mobs, regardless of distance. Any enemies they do attack won't last long due to their high attack damage.

They're useful against most enemy mobs, although they can struggle with Endermen due to the high speed of the mobs and teleporting ability. They rarely attack Creepers, and only if they have low health. They won't attack Ghasts.

Iron Golems have the highest health of any mob apart from the Ender Dragon and The Wither. You can only heal Iron Golems with splash potions, and they don't regenerate their own, so don't forget to do so if you're using them as allies in battle. They have a lot of health, but they're not invulnerable.

You may think the Iron Golem is good against the Ender Dragon and Wither, and this is often true. However, due to their very slow speed and limited attack range, they're not all that useful. When fighting the Wither, you can potentially summon the boss inside a small, enclosed room full of Iron Golems, and the cramped space means that damage will be done, but other than this, they're simply not agile enough to be of much use.

AND MING

increased by performing various actions, which contribute to the depletion of the hunger bar. Here are the various actions that cause the hunger bar to drop, in order of severity from low to high, they are:

▶ **Walking and sneaking**
▶ **Swimming**
▶ **Block breaking**
▶ **Sprinting**
▶ **Jumping**
▶ **Combat**
▶ **Taking damage**
▶ **Food poisoning**
▶ **Sprinting jump**
▶ **Health regeneration**
(with high enough hunger meter)

Food poisoning

It's not just enemy mobs and potions that can poison you, and foods can too. Some foods, when eaten, can actually cause the Hunger status effect (also known as food poisoning). This is different to actual poison (which attacks the health bar), and unlike normal hunger levels, causes the hunger bar to deplete faster, and

Hunger strikes

Food in the world of *Minecraft* doesn't restore health as you'd expect, but it instead fills up the hunger meter, which sits to the left of your health bar. This bar, when it has at least 9 full units, will allow your health to regenerate, so it's important to keep it full, especially when adventuring. If the bar runs out, your health will start dropping by half a heart every four seconds, which isn't good. On easy difficulty, your health won't drop below five hearts, and on normal it won't drop below half a heart. If you're playing on hard, though, it'll keep dropping until you're dead.

Sprinting is one of the actions that drains the hunger bar faster, but if you let it drop to six units or below, you'll be unable to sprint. This can be deadly if you don't realise and try to escape a dangerous situation and can't run.

Exhaustion levels, also called saturation, are

turns the hunger bar a yellow-green colour. Food known to cause this include rotten flesh, raw chicken and pufferfish.

Raw chicken will cause poison around 30% of the time, rotten flesh 80%, and eating a pufferfish will guarantee food poisoning. In fact, not only will pufferfish cause food poisoning, it'll also cause normal poisoning too. So, never, ever eat a pufferfish – simple.

Spider eyes and poisonous potatoes are not actually food, and eating them simply causes normal poison effects.

Best food stuffs

There are a lot of foods you can eat and prepare in *Minecraft*, but some are better than others. This isn't simply by taking into account how much they fill the hunger meter, but also their nourishment. This is the amount of saturation the foods restore. Foods with higher nourishment ensure the hunger meter lasts longer. They're best eaten when the bar hunger bar is higher, preventing excessive hunger, and ensuring you stay full for longer.

The best overall foods in the game are golden apples and carrots. Golden apples regenerate four hunger units instantly, regenerate health for around five seconds and add absorption for two minutes. Enchanted golden apples do the same, but the effects are stronger, and last longer, with regeneration lasting thirty seconds, absorption two minutes and extra bonus of resistance and fire resistance for five minutes, essential for Nether exploration.

Golden carrots have no fancy status effects, but heal six hunger units instantly per carrot. However, both of these foods are fairly difficult and expensive to craft, and so early on in the game, they're not the best to go for, for obvious reasons.

The best, most plentiful food are cooked pork chops and beef steak, as well as cooked salmon. The chop and steak fill four full hunger units, and salmon fills three. These are easy to acquire foods, at any level and have good nourishment levels.

Bread is arguably the most plentiful food, as you can grow as much wheat as you like and make masses of it. Each loaf will restore three hunger units instantly, and the nourishment is also pretty good. It's a great food, certainly for early on, and it's plentiful enough to use as a staple exploration ration.

Cake is the best food when it comes to filling your hunger bar. A whole cake fills six full units of the bar (six slices at one unit per slice). However, it also requires a lot of resources and time to make. It's also technically a block, as it needs to be placed on a surface to be eaten, so it's not all that suitable for eating when out and about. It's a great food to share with friends, though.

Mushroom stew (also called soup) could be called *Minecraft*'s super food. Each bowl restores three hunger units, and its nourishment is around the same as bread and baked potatoes. You can craft it like other foods but, and here's where the super part comes in, if you have a Mooshroom and an empty bowl, you can 'milk' the Mooshroom indefinitely, for an inexhaustible supply of mushroom stew. Simply find a Mooshroom, leash it and lead it home, and you've got a never-ending food supply.

Farming

If you're going to have plenty of food and ingredients on hand, not to mention crafting resources like wool and feathers, you're going to need to indulge your inner farmer and round up some animals. This is one of the best ways to ensure plentiful food and resources in *Minecraft*, but to capitalise on it, there are some tips you should take note of.

First, be aware of *Minecraft* spawning rules when it comes to keeping animals. You'll want

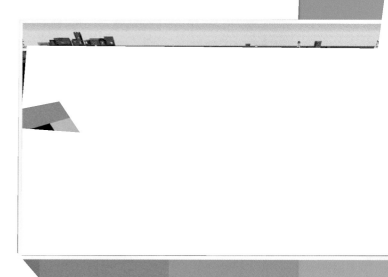

to pen in the animals with fencing or other barriers to stop them wandering off, but you'll also need to take into account the size of your enclosure. An animal cannot be allowed to move more than 20 blocks in any given direction or it'll eventually despawn. So, if you don't want to get up in the morning and see an empty enclosure, always make sure your pens are less than 20 by 20 blocks.

Animals, especially chickens, will try to escape any chance they get, and wait by gates to run free. To stop this, always build a double gate setup, so you can stop them from escaping. If they do escape, simply hold their favourite foodstuff and tempt them back. Chickens respond to seeds and Nether wart, cows to wheat, pigs like carrots (on PC, console users can use wheat), and sheep also like wheat.

Livestock uses

The four main types of farm animal are cows, sheep, pigs and chickens, and each has their own uses: cows are good for leather, meat and milk; chickens are used for meat, feathers and eggs; pigs are for meat and sheep are for wool. Cows and chickens are the most useful, and so are the best overall animals to farm, but if you need wool you'll need sheep. Pigs

may produce porkchops, one of the best foods in the game, but they're similar to beefsteak, making cows the best option.

You don't need all that many sheep, so don't waste too much space. Sheep regrow wool by eating grass, so as long as you put them on a grass surface, you'll have plenty of wool with a handful of sheep.

Breeding

Breeding is easy to do in *Minecraft*. All you need to two adult animals of the same type and some of their favourite food. Feed each animal its favourite food and love hearts will radiate from it. This is the 'love state'. Once both animals are in this state, they'll nuzzle and a baby will be born. Easy.

Chickens can also be bred by throwing chicken eggs. Each egg has a 1/8 chance of spawning a baby chick. Those that do spawn a chick also have a 1/32 chance of spawning four chicks at once.

The food to breed is the same as the food used to lure the animals. So:

Chickens = Seeds and Nether Wart
Cows = Wheat
Pigs = Carrots (Wheat on console)
Sheep = Wheat

Chickens in love mode. A baby chick is about to arrive...

Pumpkins and melons grow from vines, which need space next to farmed dirt

Baby animal can't be farmed until they're adults

Crops

Farming your own crops is the easiest way to get food, especially bread. Wheat is easy to farm, and all you need is dirt, a hoe and some seeds. Wheat crops need plenty of light, and grow quicker if next to water. Torches also provide light, and stop mobs spawning. This is important as crops can be destroyed if walked over. It's also wise to fence in your crops to stop this.

Potatoes and carrots are planted in much the same way, but use potatoes and carrots as the seeds. You can also plant melons and pumpkins on farmed land, but these require empty adjacent dirt spaces for the veg to grow on.

Sugar cane can be grown, but to do this you need to place it on a dirt, grass or sand block that's directly next to water. To avoid having to replant it all the time, when

you chop it down, always leave the bottom block of cane, as it'll simply regrow without planting.

Trees, although not a crop in the food sense, are important if you want a supply of wood. They can be planted in grass and dirt by placing a sapling. Like crops, they need light to grow, and water helps.

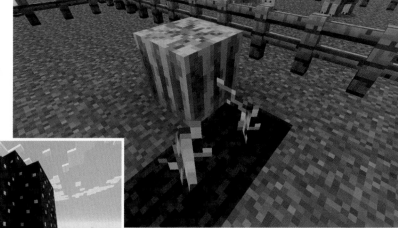

Bonemeal can instantly grow massive veggies and plants, like this giant mushroom

Bonemeal (crafted from bones) is a miracle grow item that can be applied to certain plants instantly making them grow to full maturity. Simply use the bonemeal on the crop in question. This applies to trees, wheat, potatoes, carrots, melons, pumpkins, mushrooms (which grow to giant proportions), cocoa and grass.

Wheat, carrot and potato crops, fully matured and ready for harvest

Where to Build and What to Use?

LOCATION, LOCATION

As mentioned in First Steps in a New World, it is best to begin building your first shelter as close to your original spawn point as possible. This can make it difficult to build a free standing structure like a house, as more often than not you'll spawn in thick forest, or atop uneven terrain. For this reason you may want to carve your first form of shelter out of a cliff face, cut into the side of a mountain, dig underground, or mob-proof a cave by sealing it off with stone, wood or dirt. After a while though, you may get in touch with your inner architect and build yourself a cabin, a house, a mansion or an entire town.

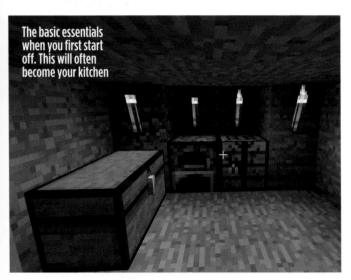

The basic essentials when you first start off. This will often become your kitchen

A HOUSE BUILT ON SAND

When building, the materials you use should be strong and fireproof. This allows you to have flammable materials including a fireplace in your home if you wish. It also protects you should a flaming zombie approach your home and from pyromaniac players lurking on the same server.

Should a Creeper pay you a visit it could obliterate anything weaker than stone or cobblestone. Materials such as dirt, sand and gravel are not very durable. Sand and gravel are also not stable and should you remove the blocks beneath them they'll fall. If sand or gravel fall on you they can cause you damage and suffocation, and if they're disturbed below you, you may find yourself falling to your doom. Sandstone is not much stronger, but does not succumb to gravity like its weaker counterpart. It is a good alternative to sand if you wish to use something of a similar style and colour for your interior.

Another important thing to note is that Endermen can move certain blocks, regardless of if they have occurred naturally, or if you have placed them yourself. The blocks they can move include grass and dirt blocks, gravel, clay, sand, mycelium (occurring instead of dirt on Mushroom Island biomes), red sand (similar to sand but occurring only in the Mesa biomes, and podzol (which is similar to mycelium, another type of dirt block and occurs in the Mega Taiga biomes.

If building with any of these materials do be prepared to find a hole in your walls or roof after an evening of frolicking Endermen. They can also place dirt blocks beside your fences, allowing mobs to breach your perimeter. They can move flowers and plants such as dandelions, poppies, blue orchid, allium, azure bluet, all types of tulip, oxeye daisies, brown and red mushrooms, cactus, pumpkin and melon blocks. For this reason you should keep a keen eye on your crops and gardens. Sometimes, when Endermen are feeling particularly pesky, they can move TNT as well, so try not to leave it out for long and if you do, check its placement before you activate it.

You may wish to use weaker materials for decoration. If you choose to do this ensure that your exterior walls are reinforced with stronger materials. For example if you wish to use wood for decoration build your exterior walls in three layers: wood, stone, wood. Some of the strongest materials to consider building with could be things like clay bricks, stone bricks, Iron if you have a lot of it, or eventually, obsidian.

HARD AS ROCK (OR OBSIDIAN):

As naturally occurring obsidian is difficult to come by, it may be a good idea to create some. You can do this by creating a cast or mould out of non flammable blocks (such as cobblestone), placing still lava in it and pouring water over the top. If you want to avoid the tedious task of mining the obsidian you make, play around with different shapes of casts or moulds and create entire walls. A simple example is to cast one wall at a time. Lay stone in a hollow rectangle two blocks high. Place a block at one end of the lower, inner hollow space. Pour a bucket of lava in each block space of the

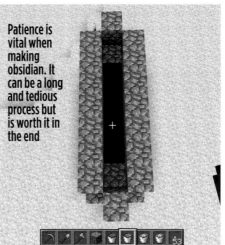

Patience is vital when making obsidian. It can be a long and tedious process but is worth it in the end

lower hollow rectangle so that the lava is still and doesn't flow. Be very careful not to fall in or touch the lava as it will do great damage and probably kill you. Standing on the highest block of your cast, aim at the stone block at the end of the lower rectangle and pour your bucket of water. Your water should flow over your still lava and turn each lava block into obsidian. Remove the water with your empty bucket by aiming in the same place you poured it (or the 'source' block). Place another layer of stone and repeat the process until your obsidian wall is at your preferred height. You do have to create your obsidian wall in layers, gradually making your wall higher but it may be easier than mining obsidian.

Once you have built an obsidian structure it is virtually indestructible. Creepers, fire, explosives, flooding, nothing can damage obsidian except a sturdy diamond pick axe. The downside is that dark obsidian walls seem to close in on you so perhaps add in a couple of picturesque windows, hang some paintings, framed items, or place torches, Redstone lamps or Glowstone to lighten your room and make one feel a little less claustrophobic. You can use obsidian as a core material and build stone, wood or brick around it, in a similar way to the wood-stone-wood method of reinforcing your walls. This allows you to make your home a little brighter and more colourful. If you like the dark look combine it with a little Netherbrick and have some fun with slabs, stairs and fences.

THROWING STONES IN GLASS HOUSES:

While glass is a great look, and can be a useful transparent block to work with due to the fact that you can look at mobs through it without provoking them (Endermen, for example) the downside is that glass is breakable. It's not much stronger than sand

and is not a renewable resource. Once you break a glass block or pane it is gone and you cannot collect and reuse it. Having said that, glass blocks and panes are a great way to brighten up a space.

Glass is made out of smelted sand, and comes in blocks which can be crafted into Glass Panes. Glass Panes are a lot more flexible and can be a creative way of decorating. It takes six glass blocks to make sixteen glass panes which are smaller than their block brethren and when glass panes are placed beside, above or below other blocks, they will change their shape to best fill the space in which they were placed. Glass panes also appear much brighter than glass blocks.

You can stain glass by crafting dye with eight glass blocks. Dyed glass blocks can then be crafted into stained glass panes in the same way that normal glass panes are made.

ATLANTIS

Underwater houses can be built with the aid of glass panes. If you are building in creative mode this will not be quite as challenging as if in survival mode, like most things. However, if playing in survival it certainly isn't impossible, just a little trickier. If you are attempting this in survival, be prepared to die a couple of times, and carry plenty of food with you to replenish your hunger and be able to heal should you get stuck under water for too long.

You can breathe underwater if standing close to glass panes. You need to start by building a path from land to the surface of water above where you wish to begin building. This allows you to place your first few panes. Glass panes are incredibly useful as you can fit through the square they make when you place four pieces together, however water cannot. Fence pieces and iron bars can be used instead of glass panes but are not quite as quickly and easily disposed of once placed. By doing this you are creating a handy way of refilling your bubble metre and catching your breath underwater. You can also do this by standing as close to glass panes as possible as they seem to form an invisible barrier very closely around them that water cannot breach.

Start building a dirt or stone pillar leading down to the underwater area you wish to build in and surround it by glass panes. When an area is filled with glass panes it eliminates the water and as long you don't break any of the outer layer it will remain a dry area, allowing you the break the glass panes inside. However, this does eliminate your ability to get back to the surface without leaving the safety of your dry interior, so have some ladders handy and place them on the stone pillar, providing you with dry means of reaching the surface.

Now you can begin using the glass panes technique to build your underwater house. Try to build room by room so you can keep track of which glass panes need to stay intact in order to keep dry. If you get stuck and cannot move, break your way out. If there is one pesky block's worth of water left in your room and you can seem to reach it to place a glass pane use an empty bucket to get rid of it or break the glass around it and use a bucket to remove the source block.

When furnishing you can do most things similarly to any other house except glass walls won't hold torches and glass floors won't hold doors. So have other sources of light or place other kinds of blocks within your home. If you wish to build your perimeter walls with something other then glass simply use glass panes as a mould and build your walls inside. When you're done just break the

The Entry to an underwater structure made entirely of glass

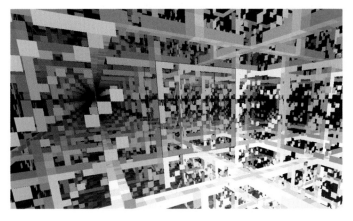

external glass. Just be sure that your inner walls are water tight before you do.

Glass houses are one of the safest way to live as there are no hostile mobs that reside underwater in *Minecraft*. Any hostile mobs you do encounter will be at the surface and no deeper. For this reason why not consider creating an underwater Atlantis for you and your friends.

Now that we've looked at what and where, let's look at how...

Basic Building

SIZE DOES MATTER

When you're working out the dimensions of your home it is a good idea to leave a little room to move. All spaces in your house should have at least three to four blocks of space between the floor and the ceiling. This allows you room to jump should you need to and provides space to place things like beds and chairs.

When building your first room it should be at least four blocks long by four blocks wide. This is so that you can put your basic essentials in there such as a Furnace, a Crafting Table and a Chest. These three items are the very basic requirements of any shelter and it is a good idea to keep them near the exit so as to make fast use of them if you're just dropping in. Eventually you may hope to put a lot in this room, and it will often become a handy kitchen. Before it does you will need to expand it to be much larger.

Hallways should be at least three blocks wide. This allows you to pass mobs, pets and players and place things along your hallway. For the same reason, stairways should be two blocks wide.

UNINVITED GUESTS

Be aware that any ceilings that are more that two blocks high may allow Endermen to teleport into your home. They'll generally only do this at night time. If you're asleep you will be none the wiser and they will not attack you. If it begins to rain outside though and they are seeking shelter you may find your living room filled with unexpected tall, dark and not-so-handsome guests until the rain stops. You can attempt to avoid this by placing a lot of light in your home, however, this will not always deter them. It does prevent them spawning within your home. (Note that spawning is different to teleporting in that an Enderman can teleport wherever it fits after it spawns but will only spawn under dark, dry conditions, in pairs or groups.)

It is usually a good idea to build a fence or wall around your property. By doing this you're ensuring that mobs cannot greet you at your door as you leave your property. You can use wood or Netherbrick fence, iron bars, or even build a sizeable wall and make your property look like a stylish fortress. Be aware that these methods do not stop spiders from finding their way into your yard and onto your roof. If you have a flat roof spiders will almost always hang out up there at all times of the day. You can prevent this by placing a lip or overhang around the edge of your roof. Do this by placing blocks, stairs or fence pieces along the very edge of your roof. This stops the spiders in their tracks and as they cannot fit in spaces less that two blocks wide you only need to place a block in every second block space in order for this to work. You can also place cacti pieces, lava or torches as spiders take damage. They won't kill a spider straight away though, and may allow a spider past without killing them, so be cautious if

An Endermen moving a block of gravel around. This could prove fatal if he decides to move the wrong block

relying only on these methods. If placing cacti, the pieces cannot be placed beside each other so leave one block space between each cacti column. Cacti can only be placed on sand and will usually not grow more than three blocks high but if you collect some you can add an extra block or two to further ensure that spiders cannot cross.

(For more ideas on how to defend your home check out our Defending Your Home tips.)

KITCHEN

As well as the basic kitchen furniture such as a work bench, a furnace, and a couple of chests, you can add decorative furniture such as a dining table and chairs, cupboards and a fridge. Dining tables can be built using upside-down stair pieces, fence pieces with pressure plates or carpet pieces on top or by using extended pistons. Carpet pieces or blocks tend to look as though you have a dining table with a table cloth when using different colours.

Cupboards are easily done by placing slabs, different coloured blocks or even book case blocks and placing trap doors on them. If you line them up one block above your bench spaces and furnaces you can make them look quite convincing. If you wish to create an ornate range hood you can use upside-down stair pieces above your furnace. Create a bench top by placing pressure plates atop blocks lined up side by side.

A fridge can be created by either placing iron blocks, quarts blocks or coloured wool blocks on top of each other and placing a button as the handle. To make a functioning fridge you may wish to cover the front of a few stacked chests or dispensers with an iron door. It is also quite simple to create a chequered floor effect using different coloured blocks or carpets.

Finally, place a couple of flower pots with plants or flowers in them to make your kitchen look a little more homely.

LIVING ROOM

Couches are easily crafted using stair pieces. As they are flexible, if you place one in the centre and one either side facing the centre piece they become corner stair pieces, making the arms of your couch. If you wish to you can simply place signs on each side of stair pieces, or some slabs, as your arms. To create large, bulky couches use blocks as the arms and back of your couch and slabs as the seats. Using this method allows you to use different coloured wools and mix and match your colours with your décor.

Use slabs or blocks as coffee tables or you can use the pressure plate on a fence post method as side tables beside your couches, again replacing pressure plates with carpet pieces as if they are adorned with a coloured table cloth.

Televisions can be created in many different ways, all varying in style and functionality. If you simply place a few black wool blocks atop some glass blocks and place bookshelves up either side, you have a nice TV Cabinet. You can use a particular painting on the wall as a wall mounted television, or for more functional televisions you can use a map, or clock in an item frame, as these things move. You can place all manner of mobs behind glass panes covering a cavity you have made in your wall. Most mobs will remain there indefinitely making for quite an interesting television. If you have a few skeleton skulls to spare they can look a lot like gaming consoles when placed around your television on a shelf or at the base of your television.

Fire places can vary in size and function. You can make a large, hollow chimney, complete with spider webs, and a huge ornate fireplace at its base using blocks, slabs and stair pieces. Or you may wish to build yourself a simpler version by placing blocks against an existing wall.

For a more modern fireplace you can place blocks leading down from the roof in the centre of your living room and use slabs or stair pieces at its base making a rim. Below you place a pit of lava or lit Netherrack and surround it with slabs or iron bars so you can't accidentally wander into it. Netherrack will provide you with animated flames and smoke, whereas lava will simply glow and bubble occasionally. You can also use glow stone or torches. While not quite as convincing, they are much safer.

Lamps can be created using Glowstone, or Redstone lamps on top of fence posts or iron bars. If using Redstone don't forget to provide a source of Redstone to power it or even lead a trail of Redstone from your lamp to a switch in the wall and create a functional lighting display.

Try adding a few plants to your room using flower pots or planter boxes. A planter box can be created by placing trap doors on each side of a dirt block and placing your plant on top. This is a handy alternative for those plants that cannot be placed in flower pots if you want them on display inside your home. You can also use uncut wood blocks topped with a couple of leaf blocks to create house plants and hedges.

Place carpet in different shapes around your living room to act as rugs and place some paintings. Get creative with item frames and frame some flowers or weapons to create lovely centre pieces for above the mantle of the fireplace.

BEDROOM

You can create an array of different bed types. Using functional beds you can place two beside each other to make a double bed for two players. Put them on top of a platform made of blocks and stairs or slabs, and place fence posts or iron bars at each corner to make a four poster style bed.

Play with different blocks and fence pieces to create a bed head. If you simply want your bed to look nice, you can create different colour combinations using wool blocks and carpet pieces. Wool blocks will not function as a bed. They are simply for display.

Bunk beds can also be created. Simple bunk beds are easily created by placing your first bed against the wall, placing two blocks at least one block above it and placing another bed on top of the two blocks. Get rid of the blocks and you have a bunk bed. Place a ladder up the wall on one or both sides to allow you safe access to the top bunk. Always ensure that both beds have at least two blocks of free space above or you will get stuck in a wall and suffocate when you wake up.

A more extravagant bunk can be made using fence posts and blocks as bed frames and posts. You can also place your bed in a hole in your floor and surround it with slabs to look a little more modern.

Place Glowstone or Redstone lamps either side of your bed or a couple of chests or bookshelves as bedside tables.

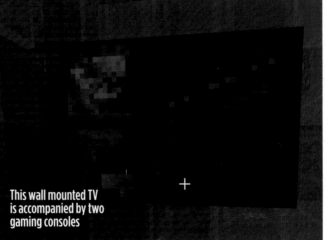

This wall mounted TV is accompanied by two gaming consoles

Create a built-in wardrobe by taking two by two blocks out of the wall and placing single chests atop each other on one side and a two block tall painting on the other as a full length mirror. Place two wooden doors over the opening and you have your wardrobe.

For Drawers you can stack blocks or double chests atop each other. If you use blocks place signs on the front with 'o' to make the handle, or use buttons.

Place some more house plants and even an en suite bathroom, along with some paintings and windows and you have a fairly impressive boudoir.

BATHROOMS

Bathrooms can be a great room to get creative in. They look especially convincing if you use a lighter coloured block like quarts for your walls and floors. Quarts and other various blocks can look like tiles, especially if you're using one of the custom texture packs available.

To create a toilet you can use a hopper or a cauldron placed in front of two blocks stacked on top to make the cistern. Place a button on the side which can be used to lift the lid and or the toilet paper and you have yourself a loo.

When creating your sink you can simply use a cauldron or hopper again and place a block either side as cabinets or a basin. Tripwire hooks make for excellent taps or you can use a lever switched down. Place buttons either side for tap handles and place a bucket of water in your sink.

For a shower you can cordon off a corner of your bathroom with glass panes or blocks. If you leave a one block wide opening and place a pressure plate on the floor, water will not pass it so you can aim at the block you want your water to pour from, pour a bucket of water and it will be contained in your shower without flooding the whole room. If you wish to have a dry shower simply place a downward facing lever or tripwire hook and some

Make your bed look like a classic four poster with a canopy using fence posts

buttons for effect and you have your shower.

Infinite water sources come in very handy around your home and can be created in many ways as well. The simplest is to create a four by four hole in the floor and pour a bucket of water in one corner, then another in the corner opposite. Once water is still and no longer flowing the water source becomes infinite. This can prove very useful when building yourself a bath tub. When doing so, you can do this with a one by three block hole, but if you do take water from it only take water from the middle block or it will disrupt the water and flow again.

You can create bath tubs in many ways. The simplest is to dig a hole in your floor however many blocks wide you wish your bath to be and simply fill it with water. You can decorate it by surrounding it with slabs to elevate the side a little bit. If you wish to create a larger, more unique bath tub you can use stair pieces in a square or rectangle. Fill in the centre with water if you wish and even add some lights under the water by way of Glowstone or torches below glass blocks to light the water. Add a tap and some handles and you have your bath.

Finally, add some bath mats in by placing coloured carpet in small areas of your bathroom floor. You can even place some wool blocks in the wall to look as though towels hang there.

STUDY/LIBRARY

This can be a cosy corner of your living or bedroom, or you could designate an entire room. While bookshelves look great in most rooms of your home, they add warmth to a study/library.

You can line the walls with bookcases and shelves by stacking shelf blocks up in columns and connecting them with slab pieces to create shelves.

Place upside-down stair pieces together to make yourself a handsome desk and place another stair piece in front as your chair. Add an iron block on top with either a painting, a sign, or an item frame on the front and this can make for a convincing computer monitor. Alternatively you can create two flat screen computer monitors if your desk is against a wall by placing two sign pieces. Type some symbols and computer jargon on them before you place them to make them look like monitors. Add piece of powered rail and a button to make for a handy keyboard and mouse.

A bathroom complete with bath, shower, toilet, and sink

POOLS

Pools can be a charming addition to any home. Whether indoor or out, round or rectangle, they are fun to design and surround by pool side furniture. Pools can be a simple rectangle, two rectangles adjoining, round, or square. Round pools can be tricky to dig as the *Minecraft* world comprises of squares. But if you think outside the box (no pun intended) you can create any shape you like.

An easily achieved exotic design is the rectangle on rectangle look. First you dig out your area and line the bottom of both rectangles with your block of choice. Lapis lazuli can look especially nice and sandstone can make the edges look nice and bright. Place a few blocks of Glowstone in the bottom and sides of your pool, perhaps behind some stained glass panes to create an elegant underwater ambiance. Once you're done and its time to fill your pool remember to have an infinite water source nearby. If your pool is quite large it can be tricky to fill so that your water is still and not flowing. One way to achieve this is to pour a bucket of water on the inside edge of each block outlining your pool. You may need to do this a few times until the water flows as far towards the centre of each rectangle as it can. Then, line your pool with blocks just below the waters surface. Cover the entire area of the pool until the water is still and not flowing. When its still you have an infinite water source in the shape of your pool and all you need to do is get rid of the blocks below the surface for it to fill the pool and remain still water.

You may wish to consider making the water level of one of your rectangles higher than the other and filling them both separately. If you do this you can the knock out the wall dividing the two rectangles to create a waterfall. Add a fancy spa (in a similar technique to how you would build a bath tub) and a few sun beds using stair pieces and slabs. You can even add a table and chairs with a large outdoor umbrella over the top using slabs, blocks and fence pieces. Finally surround your pool area with fencing, iron bars or wooden blocks topped with leaf blocks and even some wooden planks to create decking.

Some additions you may wish to add are a free standing waterfall. This can be achieved by creating a hollow wall about three blocks high. Fill with water until the water is still. Then knock out blocks from where you wish the water to flow. You can also experiment with building bridges or rooms over your pool and using glass blocks or panes so that your view out to the pool is uninterrupted. You may also wish to build a diving board or two.

ADVANCED CRAFTING

Once you've mastered the basics of crafting, you'll find that there are hundreds of additional items to create. Some can be crafted using your own two hands, but the vast majority require the use of a crafting table. In this section we'll look at some of the more interesting and useful items you can create, although you'll doubtlessly find many more recipes that we simply don't have space for – we've tried to concentrate on those which have unexpected or beneficial uses you might not discover...

The Essentials

Here are a few we like to keep close to us at all times:

Chests

Created out of nine blocks of planks arranged with an empty square in the centre, chests are used to store any item you can carry in your inventory. A single chest can store 27 items,

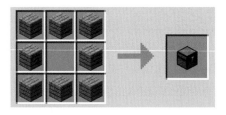

and two placed next to one another will create a double-chest with twice the capacity. Use multiple chests to organise your various resources.

Beds

Arguably the most essential item you'll craft outside of the initial tools and armour, beds are created by combining three blocks of wool with three planks. You can use any colour wool and any type of wood, but the resulting bed will always look the same. The important quality of beds is they when slept in, they create a new spawn point – thereafter

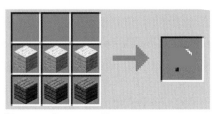

if you die, you'll return to the most recent bed you slept in (as long as it still exists).

Buckets

It'd be almost as hard to play the game without buckets

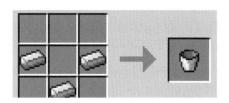

as it would without a shovel. Buckets can be created by placing three iron ingots in a V shape, then used to collect and place source blocks for water and lava. You can also use buckets to milk cows.

Doors

You can make a door by

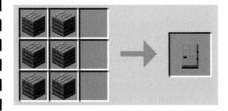

arranging six blocks of wood or iron in a vertical rectangle on the left of a crafting matrix. Wooden doors can be opened and shut by hand, while Iron Doors must be paired with a button or other on/off mechanism. Even wooden doors won't catch fire and most mobs can't open them (though villagers can). Zombies are attracted by closed doors and will attempt to break them down.

Slabs & Stairs

Most building materials can be crafted into slabs and stairs using the same technique. Three units of an item on the bottom row of a crafting matrix will create a slab, and six units in a triangular pattern (as shown) will create stairs. As well as being fun decorative

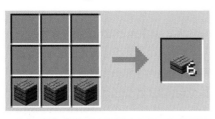

items, slabs and stairs allow players to walk the height of a single block without jumping. Staircases are more compact, while slabs can be used to make longer staircases with a more gentle incline.

Boats

Swimming in *Minecraft* is pretty much a last resort. It's slow,

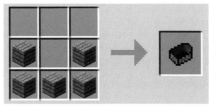

difficult and dangerous. By comparison, speeding around in a boat is great fun and helps you move even faster than on land. Placing five blocks of any wood in a U shape on the crafting matrix will allow you to build a boat, which can then be placed in water and ridden. When boats break, they will convert into oak planks, which means you can use them to convert wood into oak (if inefficiently – they drop less wood than it takes to make them).

Navigation Items

There are three items you can use to help you navigate in *Minecraft*, and we suggest creating them at the earliest opportunity.

A compass is formed by surrounding a piece of redstone with four iron ingots,

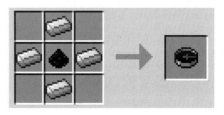

and will help you find the original spawn point for your world: the arrow on a compass always points towards it.

The same recipe with gold will create a clock, which is useful for determining whether it's night or day above ground or checking at a glance how long it is until night falls.

Surrounding a compass with paper will allow you to craft an Empty Map (although beware that you'll lose the compass!). Empty Maps are automatically filled when you look at them, and larger, more "zoomed out" maps can be created by surrounding a non-empty map (rather than a compass) with paper.

Anvils

Creating new tools and weapons all the time can get tiresome, especially if you've got one with a good enchantment that you'd rather keep. Created from four iron ingots and three iron blocks, Anvils allow you to combine partially-used tools to replenish their health and repair enchanted tools so that you don't lose the abilities they have. You can also use anvils to

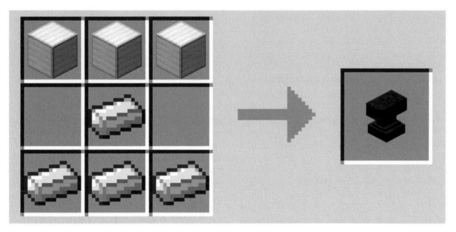

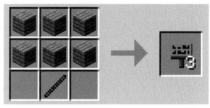

rename weapons and tools and, if you're a comedian, as the component in a trap – they're one of the few items in the game that are affected by gravity!

Flint & Steel

Did your mother ever tell you not to play with matches? Well, now you don't have to, because a flint and steel (created, unsurprisingly, using flint and an iron ingot) can start a fire instantly. Ideal for clearing dead wood, live wood and houses you don't like, even if the people are still inside them. You can also use them to create temporary light sources or, in a pinch, as an offensive weapon. Keep yours close by at all times.

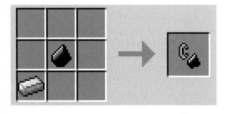

Ladders

Combining 7 sticks in an "H" shape will create 3 pieces of ladder that can be used to climb up walls or down vertical drops. One thing you might not be aware of is that you can double the effect of a ladder

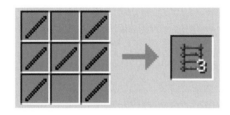

by mounting each unit a block apart. Players are tall enough to grab onto the rungs without falling, so you can make great savings (even though it looks a bit rubbish!)

The Unexpectedly Useful

Some items you can craft might seem useless, but have unexpected benefits that smart players can make use of!

Signs

Make a sign by combining six planks with a single stick. Signs can be placed on the ground or affixed to walls and chests, allowing you to create labels, warnings and navigational aids. Thanks to the free text input, there's almost no limit to what you can use signs for.

Shears

One of the lesser-used tools, shears are created by placing one ingot in the bottom left cell of a crafting matrix and one in the centre. They have a number of unique effects: they can be used to collect leaves, dead bushes, tall grass and vines, they ensure you collect the maximum available wool from a sheep (without killing it) and they can be used to break cobweb, tripwires, leaves and wool quicker than any other item.

Mineral Blocks

It's possible to craft certain mined resources into a mineral block. These are single-colour blocks comprised entirely

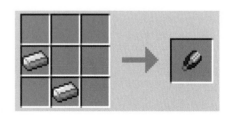

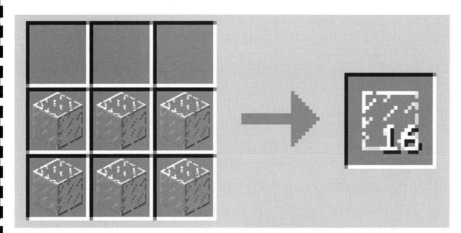

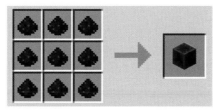

of one material, which can be placed in the world for use a decoration or storage. Typically, any mined resource that isn't already a block can be compressed into one by placing a unit of the resource in each slot of a crafting table. At present, mineral blocks can be made out of iron, gold, diamond, emerald, redstone, lapis lazuli and coal.

Since mineral blocks are stackable, you can use them to save space in your inventory. One inventory slot can store 64 iron ingots or 64 iron blocks, which are the equivalent of storing 576 ingots. When mined mineral blocks will remain as they are, but you can use a crafting table to break them back down into their component parts.

Other Compact Blocks

A large number of resources can also be compressed into compacted blocks,

although unlike mineral blocks the process is typically one-way. Compacted blocks only require four units of material to create and can be composed of the following items to creat the item in brackets: Glowstone Dust (Glowstone Block), String (Wool), Snowballs (Snow Block), Bricks (Brick Block), Stone (Stone Bricks), Nether Bricks (Nether Brick Block), Sand (Sandstone), Sandstone (Smooth Sandstone) and Nether Quartz (Quartz Block).

Glass Panes

You can create panes of glass by crafting together six glass blocks in the bottom two rows of a crafting table. They act the same as fences, so can also be used to hold back lava, water and mobs.

Item Frames

Item frames are created using a piece of leather surrounded by sticks, and have similar behaviour to a painting. While paintings are used solely as decoration, item frames are used to hang items on walls, and you can place weapons and other goods inside them. You can therefore use item frames as quick storage, allowing you fast access to items you might otherwise have to sort through a chest to retrieve.

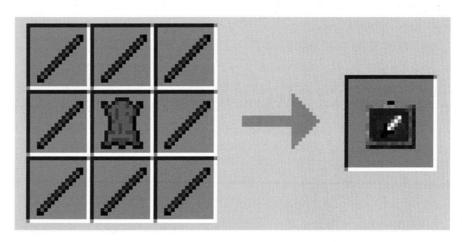

BASIC COMBAT

If you're going to survive in the world of Minecraft, you'll need to brush up on your fighting abilities

Swords

Swords are the primary weapon in *Minecraft*, and the one that you'll be wanting to use the most. They do the most melee damage and are the only weapon/tool that can block. Like all tools in the game, the material a sword is made from determines the overall effectiveness, with wood being the weakest and diamond being the strongest.

Blocking with a sword negates around half the damage dealt by an attack, so don't overlook this when heading into battle.

Bow and arrow

The primary ranged weapon is the bow, which is used to attack from afar, and the longer you hold down attack, the more range and power your arrows will have. Arrows also have a good knockback upon contact with a foe, so you can easily knock foes off ledges and into water. Arrows are

The sword is your weapon of choice for the most part, always have one ready

The bow and arrow is essential for certain foes, including the dangerous creeper

affected by gravity when they're fired, so take this into account and aim above your target for longer shots.

Tools

Although not ideal, you can use shafted tools to attack your foes (pickaxe, axe and spade), with the axe being the most effective. It's best to avoid using spades, however, as their damage is negligible, and pickaxes are far too valuable as mining tools. Axes are for chopping wood, but as they do more damage, this is the tool, if any, you should use against enemy mobs.

Hands

If all else fails you have your fists, although attacking mobs with them is not advised, and running away is a far better option. Fists will do around a quarter of the damage the weakest, wooden sword can do, so going up against foes opens you up for plenty of pain. Don't even think of trying to take on a creeper with your fists.

No gold

Gold, although good for enchantments, is one of the most useless ores to use when it comes to combat. Although you can make tools, weapons, and amour from the precious metal, it's one of the weakest, especially when it comes to weapons, so don't waste it.

Critical strike

The strength of your attacks is mainly determined by the tool used, but you can also augment this attack with a critical strike. This is done by attacking an enemy whilst falling after a jump or a drop (it won't work if you're jumping upwards). If successful, you'll see star-shaped particles appear and your foe will be knocked back. This attack can do up to 50% more damage than the normal attack.

Retreat!

It's not cowardly to beat a hasty retreat if you're in over your head, and indeed, this technique is actively encouraged when up against some enemies, such as the always-deadly creeper. If you take too much damage, or you simply don't feel you're skilled enough to tackle a foe, especially if you're in a precarious locations or on dangerous ground, then run away. Avoiding combat is a valid tactic in *Minecraft*. Running away and surviving to fight another day is preferable to losing that diamond pickaxe, so don't think twice.

Cobwebs

If you do need to retreat and have some cobwebs on hand, these can be very useful. Mobs move slowly through cobwebs, so run backwards and throw some on the ground to slow down your pursuer. Unlike soul sand, which needs to be placed, cobwebs can simply be dropped, making them the slow trap of choice in this situation.

Stay away

If you can avoid combat entirely, you'll often be better off (unless you're purposely hunting mobs for resources). Some mobs will only attack when provoked, such as spider during the day and zombie pigmen, and others can only see so far. Creepers, for example, will only attack if you get within a 16 block radius. Stay out of that, and they'll leave you alone.

Take the high ground

Most mobs need to get up close and personal to do damage to you, so use this to your advantage. If you can get to higher ground, even if it's only two or three blocks. You should be able to crouch and hit an enemy or use your bow, but they won't be able to attack you. Creepers can still be a problem, though, so always be careful.

Hit and run

We'll look at advanced and enemy-specific combat tips later, but a general, basic attack strategy is hit and run. Run in, hit your foe, then retreat. Rinse and repeat until the enemy mob is dead. This is essential against zombies and creepers, and you should get used to using it.

DEFENDING YOUR HOME

As anyone who's played *Minecraft* for more than 20 minutes well knows, night time is when the monsters come out. And as anyone's who's survived their first night'll say, the best way to stay alive is to find shelter.

It doesn't end there, of course. Soon after you'll be building yourself a better shelter, then a house or fort, and from there wherever your imagination takes you. But the problem remains: how do you protect it from the monsters that spawn every night?

The following list of tips runs from basic defensive measures to more complex and resource-intensive methods of protecting your home and possessions from the monsters of *Minecraft*.

1. Keep your home well-lit

It should go without saying that monsters don't like light and therefore won't spawn near it! Given this, it's essential to make sure that your home is well-lit, either with torches or more exotic materials and objects.

This applies to both the interior and exterior of your home. It's advisable to have light sources ringing your entire home to discourage monsters from spawning on your front doorstep.

2. You can't overlook a good wall

A simple two-block wall or ditch is efficient at keeping most monsters away from your home. The majority of monsters can only jump over heights of one block and similarly short distances horizontally, so a wall of this height will keep creepers, zombies and skeletons out.

The big exception are spiders, which can jump two blocks high, three blocks wide and even climb up walls! Fortunately there's a limitation to the spider's climbing ability: they can't climb across ceilings. If you build your walls with an outward-facing

A little elevation helps keep you safe from most monsters

Having an escape route as a backup plan may be a sensible idea

overhang, they'll be unable to get over the top of your wall.

3. A good offence is a good defence

Although passive defences like lighting and walls are effective much of the time, ensuring that you're not defenceless is the best way to ensure your ongoing survival. This applies to home defence as much as it does to mining expeditions!

Always wear armour – even weak leather armour can be the difference between life and death – and ensure you've got at least one back-up weapon. Even the best sword will break eventually.

4. I'll always be one rung above you

Ladders are rather excellent because only players can climb them. Monsters are left staring blankly at the confusing wooden object before them, unable to puzzle out its purpose. Meanwhile, you're making your escape to a nice safe tower overhead.

Be warned, though! As previously noted spiders can climb and will pursue you upwards, or if you reach a ladder and start climbing too slowly a creeper may still have time to self-destruct – blowing you and your escape route to smithereens.

5. Watch out for uninvited guests

No matter how good your defenpces are you can cause yourself problems if you don't check who's following you, or leave doors ajar.

Many's the time a player has headed back home as night falls, unaware of the creeper following them until they pause to check the view from outside their home. It doesn't look any better with them smeared up the walls.

As for leaving doors open, well, that's as good as inviting the zombies in.

6. Build a Watch Tower

Having an elevated point from which you can oversee your

home is invaluable. Not only can you check the enemies that have appeared around your perimeter, you can verify that nothing dangerous has made its way inside. You can also examine your defences from on high and check for possible gaps or vulnerabilities.

Just ensure you don't accidentally eyeball an enderman, lest your watch tower suddenly become more crowded. You can avoid that unpleasant scenario by putting glass windows in – endermen don't seem to mind if you watch them from the other side of a simple pane of glass.

7. Now you see it, now you don't

If you're playing on hard mode, be warned that zombies can break down wooden doors. This can prove fatal very quickly if you've managed to attract the attention of more than one or two enemies.

Fortunately there's a simple way to protect yourself in this eventuality. Simply replace

You can enjoy a good view in safety from a well-constructed watch tower

Just because a watch tower is functional doesn't mean it can't be stylish too

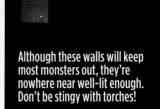
Although these walls will keep most monsters out, they're nowhere near well-lit enough. Don't be stingy with torches!

the two blocks above your door with sand or gravel and when the door's destroyed these blocks will fall, plugging the gap. It may not look aesthetically pleasing but at least nothing will be trying to chew on you.

8. Iron Doors are zombie-proof

The title says it all: iron doors are virtually indestructible by monsters and even take a long time for players to destroy. They can only be opened and closed using pressure plates or switches, however, so make sure that your door is easily operable by you.

As hundreds of horror films have taught us, there's nothing more embarrassing than being killed whilst fumbling for the door handle.

9. Use the right materials for the job

Good old-fashioned cobblestone is a dependable material for all building projects early-on, as it's such a common by-product of mining and stone is so common. It's also more resistant to damage than dirt or sand, meaning creeper explosions do a little less damage.

As time goes by you're likely to start using rarer and more aesthetically pleasing materials around your home. This is all well and good but make sure you build sensibly. Placing a wooden wall within a few blocks of a trench filled with lava is only going to end badly.

There are only a few materials more resistant to explosions than stone, cobblestone or brick, and of those only a few are practical to build with. Obsidian is the most effective, being almost impossible to destroy with explosions, but it's hard to come by in vast quantities. Water and lava are surprisingly blast resistant, however, so a cobblestone wall with water flowing over the top is almost creeper-proof.

10. They fight so that you don't have to

Don't overlook the value of a good sentry. Although expensive to build, golems are effective warriors. It's cost-prohibitive to place them everywhere but you could station them at key points around your home, or even place just one in a courtyard and lead intruders toward them.

Cats are also good sentries; they won't fight enemies but there's nothing that scares a creeper more than a cute little kitty. That's right, the scourge of the night will turn and flee when it sees a cat.

11. Trench warfare

Digging a trench and filling it with deep water or lava is an effective way of killing anything wandering toward your home. Enemies can drown in water over time and will die in lava almost immediately – although lava will also destroy any items they might drop.

It's possible to set up sloping trenches filled by moving water currents as a means of drowning attackers and washing the items they drop into a chute that deposits these leftovers somewhere safe for you to collect. It's a lot more involved than just digging a moat, but it certainly helps you collect more resources in the long run.

12. Get creative!

Once you reach the point in *Minecraft* that you've plenty of resources to play with, you'll be able to experiment with different kinds of defences. How about a landmine, for example? Just top a block of TNT with a block of sand and a pressure plate, and hey presto: that creeper's on the receiving end of a nasty surprise. It's possible to set up complex redstone circuits that trigger piston or arrow traps, or extend and withdraw drawbridges.

As you play more of the game you'll learn about the unique properties of each type of block and items – and you'll often find they can be turned effectively to home defence!

VILLAGERS & SIEGES

Buildings to be found in Villages

Villages appear quite frequently. They appear in only three biomes – Plains, Savanna and Desert – as they require reasonably expansive open spaces in order to spawn. Fortunately these three biomes are all common, so no matter where you find yourself a village will not be too far away.

Villages are populated by non-hostile Villagers, with the number of buildings in the village dictating how many villagers are present. As with everything in *Minecraft* simple arithmetic underlies this, but suffice to say even the smallest village will feature a well, a house and a villager. There is no limit on how large a village can be, but in practical terms the game will stop generating more buildings after a point.

There are eight types of building that can spawn in villages: huts, large and small houses, smithies, churches, farms, libraries and butcher's shops. Huts are crude whereas small houses are much the same size but are made of different materials. Large houses are the main form of dwelling for villages, and tend to appear in an 'L'-shape.

Of the non-home types of building, the smithy is the most sought after. Inside every smithy is a chest containing a randomised selection of items. These may include low-value objects such as bread, apples and saplings or rare items such as obsidian, diamonds or even horse armour.

At present butcher's shops and libraries don't have much to distinguish them: they look unique, with the former featuring a small pen for animals and the latter including bookshelves and a crafting table, but there's nothing else special about them and animals don't necessarily appear in the butcher's pen. Villagers don't seem to mind parts of their buildings being damaged, however, so if you want bookshelves you could always 'borrow' some!

Churches are taller than any other villager building and are therefore useful as look-outs. Farms can also prove useful, as they grow fourteen blocks of crops which the player can harvest and re-plant.

Plains villages are the most commonly encountered

Types of Villager

The five different types of villager correspond to the different buildings that can appear. You can find Farmer villagers, Blacksmith villagers, Butcher villagers, Priest villagers and Librarian villagers. They wear different coloured robes: light brown, dark brown, light brown with a white apron, purple and white respectively.

You'll only find villagers of a certain profession in a village featuring a building that matches that job. As a result, small villages will only contain one or two types of villager, and you may have to seek out a larger or even multiple villages to find the type of villager you want.

Each type of villager offers up different items for trade. For more on village trading, see the next section in this book!

There are two other 'types' of villager you may encounter: children and iron golems. These special cases will be covered over the next few pages.

Churches are a great spot to keep look out from

Interacting with Villagers

Villagers will never leave their village: they won't even stray too far from it. However, that doesn't mean they won't wander somewhere stupid: off a cliff, into a cavern, into lava, etc. Sometimes player intervention is required to help keep them safe, for example by building a fence or wall between a village and a sheer drop.

The focus of a village is always the well, so if you're wondering where to build a fence, use that as your central point. Villagers won't travel more than 64 blocks away from their village's well.

Players have a certain level of popularity with each village, which starts at zero and can be changed based on how the player interacts. It should come as no surprise that attacking or killing villagers and especially their children doesn't endear you to them! However, you can improve your popularity with them by making certain trades - see trading section for more.

Villagers will also breed to increase the local population so that it meets the maximum allowed by the village's size. At least two villagers will be needed to permit this to happen (I don't think this fact should surprise anyone). Mating produces village children, who take about 20 minutes to mature to adulthood. In the meantime, they run about a lot and get underfoot.

Walls make for good basic defences

Zombie Sieges

You and the friendly villagers of *Minecraft* are both vulnerable to monster attacks – and sometimes a zombie siege might break out.

If enough zombies spawn within or close by a village then a siege will be triggered, and the newly-formed zombie horde will begin attacking. However, a village needs at least ten buildings and around twenty villages for a siege to occur naturally.

It's important to bear in mind that special rules apply to zombies

Zombie Behaviour

The first thing to take into account is how zombies behave. Although light levels don't affect zombie spawning during a siege, it is possible to leave an area dark in order to encourage zombies to spawn there. This means you can 'channel' them through a specific route and place traps or sentries there, or set yourself up to fight off the undead menace.

Zombie hordes will generally try and attack the closest villager; if no villagers are present, they'll switch to attacking the doors to buildings that villagers are hiding inside. If you're playing on easy or normal they shouldn't be able to break these doors down, but on hard it won't take them long to break through.

At night all is peaceful...
or so it seems

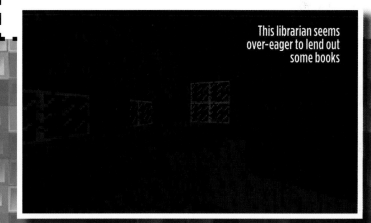

This librarian seems
over-eager to lend out
some books

spawning around villages when a siege occurs. Light levels don't affect them – they can appear right in the middle of a village, or even inside a building! All they need is sufficient space to spawn.

Fortunately, there are a number of ways to make defending villages from zombie sieges rather easier. Some involve exploiting zombie and villager behaviour, whilst others draw on mechanical know-how and cunning traps. Of course, you could also use both.

Sieges

There are a couple of very easy ways to prevent zombie sieges: The first method is to ensure you sleep through the night when close by the village. Zombie sieges typically trigger at midnight, although ordinary monster spawns near the village can still attack before then. The second is to stay more than 128 blocks away from the village when active at night. This can be tricky when mining, as you may not know how far you are from a village, but when on the surface it's much easier to judge. Essentially, zombie sieges won't occur if the player is not near by or awake. Use this to your advantage.

Defending against Sieges

Larger villages should spawn with an iron golem, which won't attack you unless provoked or you've been killing villagers. Golems will attempt to kill zombies but they can only take on so many. You can however bolster their numbers with extra golems of your own.

Building walls around a village and ensuring there are plenty of light sources around is a great way of keeping regular monster spawns out, although they won't be able to prevent a zombie siege entirely for reasons I've already mentioned. However, if you leave a gap in your wall and place sentries or pressure plate-triggered traps there,

It may be arid, but that doesn't seem to bother these villagers

you'll find it easier to fend off zombie sieges. Just make sure you don't make the walls so far away from the village centre that zombies begin spawning within the walls!

An effective if slightly cynical way of fighting zombies spawned in a siege is to trap a lone villager within eight fences. Zombies will tend to be drawn towards this apparently vulnerable villager, allowing you to kill them one by one.

Another method not quite within the spirit of the game is to wait until villagers have all fled indoors and then place blocks in front of their doors, preventing the zombies from reaching the doors to break them down.

Repopulating Villages & Curing Zombieism

If a village is overrun and converted into zombie villagers, it is possible to re-populate it. However, it's a lot of hard work and requires some advanced potions to boot!

If you've got your own minibar stocked with various concoctions and want to cure a village of zombieism, the first step is to brew a splashable potion of weakness and craft a golden apple (using an apple and gold ingots). Hit the zombie with the potion, feed them the golden apple, and then wait. The cure is already taking effect!

Zombie villagers are still vulnerable

Golems are tough and will aggressively attack monsters, but are friendly toward villagers

to sunlight so while the cure is taking effect you may wish to build a shelter around them or splash them with a potion of fire resistance as well. Alternatively you could lead your chosen zombie villager into an existing building, block off the doors and then hit them with the cure.

Once you've got at least two villagers they'll begin breeding again, but repopulating a large village in this way can take a very long time. We'd recommend curing four or more villagers, if possible, before you clear out any remaining zombies. After that you can leave them to their love affairs while you get on with fortifying the village defences!

VILLAGES AND TRADING

One of the quickest ways to get rare and hard-to-make items without putting in a lot of work is to trade your valuables with people around you. And the same is also true within a game of *Minecraft*. Trading with villagers adds an extra dimension to your game, as well as giving you a good reason to go looking for gems and precious metals even when you've got enough items to keep you going, and for turning common items into rarer ones!

In this section of the guide, we'll give you all the hints, tips and information you need to find villagers and get your hands on their most precious valuables. Legitimately, of course!

Villages

You can't find villagers without villages, and the first thing you have to do is recognise what a village is and where you can find one.

As defined by *Minecraft*, villages are small groups of around 3-6 buildings which can spawn in any of three different biomes: Plains, Savanna or Desert. They are inhabited by NPC (non-player character) humans who, while mute, can be interacted with on a basic level. Most importantly, by trading with them.

Villages themselves are usually constructed from simple, locally-found materials such as wood and sandstone, so there's rarely any benefit to be found in demolishing them for parts. Even if they weren't of any practical value, villages add much-needed character to *Minecraft*'s otherwise natural landscape, so they're worth keeping around for that reason alone. Philanthropic players might even want to expand them!

There are various different structures which can spawn as part of a village. As well as basic components like roads and lampposts, you'll also see a variety of buildings. Although they appear identical, you can recognise their function without too much difficulty. We've identified the giveaway features below.

Wells are basic pools of water surrounded by small structures. They are considered the centre of any village, and as such there can be only one in any locality. They otherwise serve a purely aesthetic function, although it is possible for mobs to become accidentally trapped in wells during the day which makes them excellent for gathering items that only mobs drop.

Huts are the most basic dwelling, with a rounded roof and dirt floor. They house up to one villager, although may spawn empty. If you find one without an inhabitant, why not move in?

Small Houses are slightly bigger than huts and have a flat roof and a cobblestone or

The local priest. He seems pleased to see us

A church at sunrise

The interior of a Butcher's. Seems totally not threatening, right?

sandstone floor. They may spawn with a villager attached, but since they have no door they are not considered homes for individual villagers.

Large Houses look similar to small houses, but are larger and L-shaped. They always house two farmers.

A butcher's shop contains a "counter" made of slabs as well as a seating booth made of stair blocks and a table. A fenced off yard is often attached to the rear. The building will spawn containing a butcher and up to one farmer.

Libraries look like long, narrow houses with large windows and contain mostly tables and bookshelves, although you will also find a crafting table. The building will always contain one librarian and one farmer.

Blacksmiths are some of the most complicated buildings in a village, instantly recognisable by its small porch. It also contains a Blacksmith's smelting pool (lava) and two furnaces, although the most interesting item inside is the chest, which contains a selection of common items. Blacksmiths spawn with the building, but since it has no door they are normally found wandering around the village.

Farms are easy to spot thanks to the crops planted nearby. They grow wheat, potatoes or carrots with irrigation between each row of

plants. They spawn with a farmer attached.

Finally, churches are large, tall structures with three floors. On the ground floor you'll find an "altar" made of stairs, and on the second floor you'll find a balcony (the first floor is an empty room). Churches spawn one priest and up to one farmer.

Village Tips

The hardest thing about villages is the rarity with which they spawn. The easiest place to find villages is in desert biomes, since they stick out against the yellow background and can't be obscured by trees. Get up high and search the horizon. If there's a village around, you'll quickly spot it!

Once you find a village, it's worth noting its location so you can create a "trade route". If you have a compass, you should use it to navigate back to your bed/spawn point and leave markers on the way so you can find your way back. If you're not averse to breaking character a little, you can press [F3] (on the PC) to bring up debug information which will give you the Village's X/Y/Z co-ordinates which you can then screenshot or note down.

If you're struggling to find a village, trying making a large map of your surroundings using paper and compasses. Villages have a very distinctive pattern from above, so even if you can't see one directly you should be able to locate it from the bird's eye view a map gives.

When you find a village, take care to introduce extra lighting immediately. Mobs can and will kill villagers if they can, and large houses in particular need additional lighting installed at the earliest opportunity as their interiors are dark enough for mobs to spawn. Villagers are no good to you dead!

It is possible to manually expand villages and increase the number of villagers that spawn inside them by adding extra dwellings. Broadly speaking, the chance of this happening is determined by the amount of doors you add. Each door contributes a third to a villager's chance of spawning, so 3 extra doors means a 100% chance of at least one extra villager appearing.

Remember that villages will not spawn anywhere in your world if the "Generate Structures" setting was not active! If you're struggling to find any even after exploring a wide area, this may be the case.

Inhabitants

Villagers may look slightly disturbing thanks to their bald heads, large faces and permanently folded arms, but they're actually very peaceful. That said, attacking a villager with a melee technique or weapon will activate the village's Iron Golem, which will

Well well well. This well looks well. Nicely built as well.

Trading with a villager. Emeralds for melon slices. Seems fair!

This butcher's so excited to have company that he's dancing on the table

arrive to protect it, so don't get too stab-happy with your weaponry!

Villagers only spawn in villages and will remain close to their homes, conversing with one another and going about their daily business. There are five types players can encounter: Farmers, Librarians, Priests, Blacksmiths and Butchers (this doesn't include the Zombie Villager mob).

Unlike mobs, villagers can use doors and climb ladders, and will hide in their homes if it rains or if they're attacked by zombies. When a village is attacked by zombies, the local Iron Golem will awaken to protect them. Like animal mobs, villagers will breed under the right conditions, although in this case it requires there to be empty dwellings in the village as determined by the number of wooden doors. When villagers breed, a child villager will be spawned, and after 20 minutes it'll grow into a randomly-selected class of villager. Note that only adult villagers can be traded with!

If you want to force the creation of new villagers, you can use this information to "farm" them (just don't let the Human Rights courts find out). Place two villagers inside a stone pen with a lot of wooden doors around it and watch their population grow. When the villagers reach adulthood, you can trade with them. Just don't tell us what you do with them after that.

The rear yard of butcher's shop, with a temple visible in the distance

Trading

Trading with villagers is a good way to get your hands on items that would otherwise require dangerous underground excursions. You can trade with any adult villager and will receive different offers based on their profession.

When you offer an item (or items) to a villager, they'll offer their own goods as trade. The most common currency is emeralds, but if you don't have emeralds you can get them by selling certain items in bulk to villagers depending on their profession. A butcher, for example, may sell you 6-7 cooked porkchops for a single emerald, or you can sell 14-17 uncooked pork chops to the villager to receive one emerald. The exchange rate is poor, admittedly, but it's also the only way you can convert uncooked meat into diamond tools.

Although rare, Priests are arguably the most useful trader in the game. As well as selling you an Eye of Ender for 7-10 emeralds (an item essential for making beacons, and otherwise hard to obtain) Priests may also offer to enchant items for tools and armour for you if paid 2-4 emeralds. Notably, the only way to legitimately obtain a Bottle o' Enchanting in survival mode is by trading 2-4 emeralds with a priest.

Trading in general is more complex than it initially seems, so take some time to familiarise yourself with the process. Trades and prices vary from villager to villager, even within towns, and certain trades can only be performed a limited number of times before the offer is withdrawn.

Trading Tips

While you can dig emeralds out of raw ore found in the extreme hills biome, they are incredibly rare. It's far easier to find villagers with butchers, librarians or farmers and trade common, easily-farmed items such as paper, raw meat and wool in exchange for emeralds.

Trading with a villager also increases their health. What this says about capitalism, we don't know, but it may be a useful mechanic if a village is being attacked by mobs.

Blacksmiths and butchers cannot tell the difference between coal and charcoal, and will trade the latter as the former. You can use this technique to quickly farm nearby trees into emeralds without the use of a pickaxe, although in many cases it's probably easier to simply mine for some coal!

Once a villager has picked a set of offers, they will only ever make those offers to you. If you find that villagers aren't giving you the offers you need, you can de-populate a village and breed new villagers who, when they grow to adulthood, will have a fresh set of trading offers for you. De-populating villagers can be done the old-fashioned way (if you don't mind a fight with an Iron Golem) but it's probably less hassle to use lava, fall damage or fire to kill off a villager more discreetly.

A grassland village, at night. Much more pleasant, isn't it?

MINING RARE ORES

Digging the cave

It's not hard to find ore in *Minecraft*, at least the less valuable ores. It's easy enough to find coal and iron, and you'll often stumble upon these simply walking through caves, and even out in the open. The more valuable ores, however, aren't as keen to be found.

There's no one way to guarantee you find rare ore, but if you're careful, and mine with a plan, you can greatly improve your chances.

Instead of randomly digging out mine shafts, it's better to mine one large 'trunk' shaft, and then mine smaller shafts off from this. This let's you branch out and cover a larger area than a single shaft. You can also mine out huge areas of the map, but this takes much more time and resources.

Ores will spawn at different levels, with coal and iron beginning to spawn at higher levels, and rarer ores like Diamond spawning much lower down. A good guide is to head for Y-11 (press F3 to see the debug screen,

as mentioned in our early mining tips). All ores naturally spawn at this level. Contrary to popular belief, hitting bedrock does not mean you've hit gold dust. Ores are not as plentiful at the world's core as you may think.

Isolation

When you find a vein of rare ore don't simply plug away at it with your pickaxe. Always isolate a vein before you mine it by carefully mining out the blocks around it. This is to stop any mined ore falling into lava hidden underneath (always an issue with obsidian). The ore blocks are safe until you mine them, so don't risk losing any precious resources.

Lapis Lazuli

Although not all that useful when it comes to tools, Lapis Lazuli is still a desirable find as it's used widely in dyes, and can also be crafted into Lapis Lazuli blocks. When mined it drops usable resources instantly, unless mined with the Silk Touch enchantment

Always isolate rare ores before you mine them to avoid loss due to lava

which will cause Lapis Lazuli blocks to be mined. You can mine Lapis Lazuli with stone pickaxes and above.

Lapis Lazuli will spawn below a depth of 30, and is found mostly between levels 13 and 16. Although not incredibly valuable in terms of uses, it's actually quite rare, so it's always a good idea to mine it when you find it.

Lapis Lazuli ore

weapons and tools isn't advised due to its weakness and rarity, although it is the fastest material at tasks. It's better to use gold for crafting items like compasses and powered rails, as well as making golden apples and so on.

Redstone

Probably the most plentiful 'rare' ore in the game, Redstone is everywhere, and isn't all that hard to locate, spawning in the bottom 16 layers of the map. It's commonly found within 10 blocks of Bedrock, so digging deep is the best way to find it.

You can mine Redstone with iron pickaxes and above, and it drops usable Redstone dust instantly (silk touch gains Redstone ore blocks).

Redstone is used mainly for Redstone circuits, so is an essential find for creating mechanisms. It's also used in compasses, and nine Redstone dust piles can be crafted into a Redstone block.

Gold

Gold is one of the rarer ores in the game, and whilst it has many uses, a lot of them are fairly pointless. Using gold to craft armour,

Gold ore is found in the bottom 32 layers of the world, and appears in blocks of 4-8 blocks. You can mine it with Iron pickaxes and above (not gold). Gold nuggets can also be found on Zombie Pigmen in the Nether, and nine of these

Redstone ore

can be crafted into a single gold ingot.

Diamond

Diamond is the *crème de la crème* of *Minecraft*'s ores, and the one sight every single *Minecraft* player loves to see. Diamond is, aside from emerald, the rarest block in the game, so finding it occupies much of a player's time. It's very important as it can be used to craft the strongest weapons, tools and armour, and is needed to mine obsidian, used to create portals to the Nether.

Diamond spawns very rarely in the bottom 16 layers of the map, from levels 2-15 in small veins (usually three or four blocks). It can only be mined using iron pickaxes or above, and it's a good idea to do so with a pickaxe enchanted with Fortune III, as this can sometimes yield four diamonds per block. Of course, you first need two diamonds to make an enchantment table, so you'll need to find them first before you can enchant anything.

Always, always isolate diamond veins before mining them. They're so rare that losing one to unseen lava is a nightmare.

Obsidian

Obsidian is one of the strongest blocks in the game, second only to bedrock, and as such is also the hardest to mine,

Diamond ore

when you can find it, that is. It's not as rare as diamond or emeralds, but it can still be hard to find. Its primary use is to create Nether portals, but it's also used in crafting (enchantment tables), and building due to its high blast resistance.

Obsidian doesn't actually spawn with the world, but is actually created afterwards when water comes into contact with a lava source block. The cooled lava turns into obsidian ore. This means that you'll always find naturally occurring obsidian near lava, which usually appears underground on levels 1-10.

Obsidian can only be mined with a diamond pickaxe, and as it's always encountered by lava, you should do your best to isolate it before mining, as mined obsidian blocks falling into lava will be destroyed. Of course, the lava element makes mining obsidian particularly dangerous, so it goes without saying that you should always carry a water bucket or two when you mine it, and only take the needed supplies, leaving the rest at home in the safety of a chest.

Obsidian can also be farmed by making it yourself.

Obsidian ore created by lava

First, mine the trench 2 block deep with a step at the end and fill each deep hole with lava (to make each a source block)

Now, pour a bucket of water onto the step, and the water will flow over the lava creating obsidian as it goes

Use the bucket on the water source block and then use a diamond pickaxe to mine the obsidian

To do so you'll need a number of buckets of lava, a bucket of water and a diamond pickaxe. Start by building a two block high trench around seven blocks long, with a block step at one end. Fill each block of the trench with lava, making each block a source block (still lava). Now, pour

Emerald ore is the rarest ore in the game, so don't pass up the opportunity to mine it

the water onto the raised step block and it'll flow over the lava, making obsidian. This can then be mined and you can repeat the process.

Emerald

Currently, emeralds serve only one real purpose in *Minecraft*, and that's to trade with villagers. In ore form, it's the rarest natural block in the game and you'll only find it in Extreme Hills biomes between layers 4 and 32. You'll only find it occurring in single blocks, so if you plan on hunting for them, it's best to do so with a pickaxe that has a Fortune III enchantment, as this can yield up to four emeralds per block (instead of only one with a normal pickaxe).

You can use emeralds to make emerald blocks for decorative purposes, but due to their extreme rarity, it's not wise, and they're best used for trading.

Nether Quartz

If you want to create advanced mechanisms like the daylight sensor or Redstone comparator, then you're going to need Nether Quartz (also simply called Quartz). As the name suggests, this is only found in the Nether, and it spawns on almost all layers, so you can find it just as easily on surface layers as you can if you dig.

Once smelted, Nether Quartz ore produces usable quartz, which can then be crafted with and turned into decorative types of quartz block.

FIGHTING ENEMY MOBS

Zombie

Zombies are one of the most numerous enemies in the game but not all that dangerous. In groups they can be a problem, and if they surprise you in a mine, you may be in trouble.

They attack by simply walking up to you and hitting you, so if kept at a distance, they're easy prey. Arrows are the safest way to defeat them, but arrows can be quite scarce, so a sword is best. Simply run toward them, hit them, and then move back. Repeat until they're dead (again).

Zombies spawn in darkness, and are hurt by sunlight, which will kill them. They can stop this by standing in water, rain or the shade.

Zombies can also break down wooden doors on hard difficulty, but not iron doors. Occasionally they'll spawn with armour or pick it up. This can affect their defence and attack. Helmets also make them immune to sunlight.

There are various versions of zombies, including villagers and babies, the latter of which are smaller, faster and immune to sunlight.

Skeleton

Skeletons are another common foe you'll encounter, and they're much more dangerous than zombies. They attack using bows and arrows, and are good shots. This ranged attack makes them dangerous from almost anywhere. The safest way to fight a skeleton is using arrows, seeking cover between shots. Melee is more dangerous, and you'll usually take one or two hits, but you can use the environment to shield yourself, and lure them into traps.

Like zombies, skeletons burn in sunlight and need shade or water (or a helmet) to survive. Skeletons can also hit other mobs, which will become hostile (including other skeletons). If a skeleton attacks a Creeper and kills it, a music disc will be dropped.

Creeper

The most iconic mob of *Minecraft*, the Creeper is also one of the most dangerous. They're silent, and explode when they get close

enough, usually killing you if you're not protected enough. They're great pathfinders, and unlike zombies or skeletons, don't burn in sunlight. They have a nasty habit of creeping up behind you (hence the name) and blowing you up before you know what hit you. They can demolish your home and any other weak structure.

Again, arrows are the safest way to take on a Creeper, and two or three fully powered shots will kill them. However, the most effective and less wasteful method is to use your sword. Approach the Creeper but don't get too close. Hit it and then back off quickly and let the Creeper calm down, then repeat. As long as you don't stay too close, it won't explode.

Spider
Spiders are the only mob able to climb walls, and they can be quite dangerous during the night. In the day they're neutral, and will only attack if provoked. At night, they'll come for your blood.

A sword to the face is the best method of dealing with them, as they're not all that dangerous when it comes to attack strength.

The cave spider variant, on the other hand, is very deadly, able to poison you. They're smaller and have a blue tint. They're only found in abandoned mine shafts and strongholds. If you see these and you don't have the means to cure yourself, either run away or use arrows.

Endermen
A strange mob, the Endermen are usually neutral, until you look at them, at which point they'll attack. They can teleport around the world at high speed, and they can also pick up and place blocks, including those that make up your own home.

Unless you're harvesting Eyes of Ender, which they can drop when they die, they're usually best avoided. If you do need to kill them, use a decent sword (diamond preferably) and have armour if you can. They take damage from water, so if you provoke one, lead it into water.

It should also be noted that wearing a pumpkin on your head lets you look directly at Endermen, and they won't attack.

Slime
Slimes are slow green blobs that bounce around, and they're only really dangerous if they surprise you. When attacked they split into several smaller slimes, each of which can split

which can split further. The best way to tackle a slime is to whittle it down from a distance with arrows, then wade in with your sword to finish off the smaller blobs.

Spider Jockey

Combining the attack range of a skeleton and the climbing ability of a spider, these are a Minecraft nightmare. They're very dangerous, and luckily, they're also very rare (spiders have a one per cent chance to spawn a skeleton jockey). You can damage either one of the duo independently, but it's often best to hide and wait for daylight to finish off the skeleton for you.

If you do fight them, use arrows to pick them off from distance, going for the skeleton first and, when left with the spider alone, switch to your sword.

Witch

Witches attack by throwing various splash potions at you, depending on your distance to them. They can throw potions of slowness, poison, weakness and harm, and if set on fire they drink potions of fire resistance.

Because of this attack style, arrows are the best way to combat a witch, defeating it from outside of the potion throwing range.

Magma Cube

Magma cubes are similar to slimes, and have the same general attack. Also like slimes, they split into smaller blobs when attacked. They're immune to fire and lava and are dangerous,

even in their smallest form.

Still, the same tactics apply, and you should break them down from a distance and finish them off with your sword, just taking extra care with the tiny ones.

Zombie Pigmen

These denizens of the Nether are usually neutral, which is fortunate, as they're also very dangerous when provoked, doing a great deal of damage. What's more, any pigmen in range will also turn hostile, and you could be in serious trouble.

If you need to attack them (to harvest gold nuggets or ingots for example), then do so at range with arrows. If there are other pigmen around, build yourself a little bunker to protect yourself from the oncoming onslaught.

If you don't need gold nuggets, then it's by far a better strategy to leave pigmen to go about their business.

Blaze

Perhaps the most dangerous enemy in the Nether, Blazes are a serious force to be reckoned with. They fly, they're immune to fire, and they hurl fireballs at you, which can't be blocked. What's more, they're usually only found around a monster spawner in a Nether fortress, so an endless stream of them will assault you.

Swords are not advised against blazes, as you need to get close, and you'll probably take a lot of damage. Arrows are more useful, but the Blaze's erratic movements can make them hard

to attack. Oddly, the best weapons to use against the Blaze are snowballs. They're fast to throw and do around three hearts of damage to a Blaze. You should also ensure you have potions of fire resistance if you plan on taking them on.

Ghast

Ghasts are large, flying squid-like creatures that make baby noises. They fire explosive fireballs at you, and can do so from a great range. They often fly around the Nether above lava lakes, and are immune to this lava.

Despite their size, Ghasts aren't that durable, and two or three arrows will take them down. The difficult aspect of fighting them comes from avoiding their fireballs (which also set the environment on fire) and killing them over land so you can collect the Ghast tears they drop. You can also deflect their fireballs back at them with a timed attack. If you prefer to attack from close range, use a fishing rod to pull a Ghast in.

Building a bunker or wall out of cobblestone is good tactic, as Ghast fireballs cannot destroy cobblestone (its blast resistance is enough to absorb the damage), or set it on fire.

Silverfish

Found hiding in monster eggs (which are disguised as normal cobblestone, stone, or stone brick blocks), silverfish are tiny, insect-like creatures that emerge from damaged eggs and attack the player, alerting and attracting other silverfish in the area as they do so. If not killed quickly, they'll wander off and hide again, turning a normal block into a new monster egg.

Monster eggs are only found in Extreme Hills biomes and Strongholds. If you find one, it's best to attack silverfish from atop a 2-block high tower. Silverfish won't be able to hurt you this way. You can kill silverfish by dropping buckets of lava on them, or even blocks like gravel. These non-direct attacks (no actual weapons involved), won't alert other nearby silverfish. If you use a sword, use a powerful one, like diamond, as a single hit kill also won't alert other silverfish.

Wither Skeleton

Found in the Nether, these dark skeletons are very dangerous. They wield stone swords and if they hit you, they can inflict you with the Wither curse, which damages you over time. They're more durable than normal skeletons, do a lot of damage, and are immune to fire.

Killing these is the only way to find Wither skulls, needed to summon the Wither, so if you need to kill them, be sure to do so from a distance, out of range of their Wither-casting attacks. You can fight them with swords, just use the same hit and run technique used with zombies and Creepers. This is often hard to do, however, as you'll often be fighting Blazes and other Nether foes at the same time.

NETHER PORTALS

The road to the Nether

There's much more to the world of *Minecraft* than lush green hills, snowy forests and sandy deserts, and it's not all as picturesque and postcard. There's an evil, hellish world bubbling over with lava, hidden away for keen adventurers to find, and if you're planning on getting the most out of the game, and plan to take on the Ender Dragon, you'll need to visit this place. This is the alternate dimension known as the Nether.

Filled with lakes of lava and some of the most dangerous mobs in the game, the Nether is also full of rare resources and important items. Surviving in the Nether is tricky, but before you even get there, you'll need to know how, and the road to the Nether is almost as tricky as the alternate world itself.

To get to the Nether you'll need to build a Nether portal, and for this you'll need obsidian, 10 or 14 blocks of it. You'll also need a flint and steel to activate it when its built. Of course, in order to mine obsidian, you'll also need a diamond pickaxe, and you'll need to actually find obsidian.

We've looked at how to find obsidian in our section on finding rare ore, and we've also covered diamonds. It can take a long time to find the resources, and this is why getting to the Nether is such a lofty goal. It's not difficult in itself, it just takes a lot of time and patience.

Portal building

Building a Nether portal is easy. When you've got the obsidian and a flint and steel, you simply need to use the obsidian to make the portal frame, then use the flint and steel to activate the portal. Portals can be built in

The cornered and cornerless portals, side by side

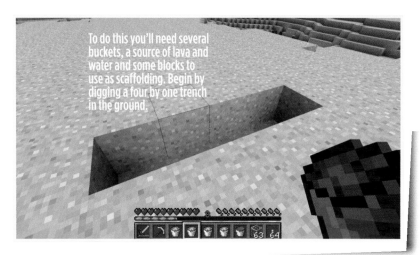

To do this you'll need several buckets, a source of lava and water and some blocks to use as scaffolding. Begin by digging a four by one trench in the ground.

Now fill the trench with lava, using a bucket of lava on each block to ensure each is a source block (still lava)

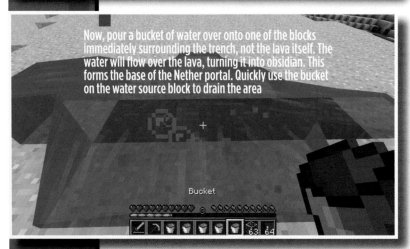

Now, pour a bucket of water over onto one of the blocks immediately surrounding the trench, not the lava itself. The water will flow over the lava, turning it into obsidian. This forms the base of the Nether portal. Quickly use the bucket on the water source block to drain the area

Bucket

Now, using some blocks (glass blocks shown here), build a one block container around one end of the base. This is the first part of the sides of the portal

two ways, with or without corners, with the former requiring 14 blocks of obsidian, and the latter only 10. A full portal with corners is four wide and four high, with a two-by-three high hole in the middle. The partial frame is the same, only missing the corners. Both are shown here.

To actually use a portal, ignite it and then step into the purple portal and wait. The screen will wobble, and after a few seconds, you'll be transported to the Nether, where a corresponding portal is created at the same time.

Shortcut to the Nether

You can speed things up by making your own obsidian (which we also covered in rare ore), but for diamonds to mine it, you're on pretty much on your own. If you're a little impatient, and want to get to the Nether without diamond tools there are ways, perhaps the best being to cast portal out of lava.

Mobs and Portals

Once a portal is built, it's not only you as the player who can use it for travel. As well as being able to send items and vehicles through, enemies and other mobs can also venture to and from the Nether. On higher difficulties, zombie pigmen will also spawn in the overworld around the portal. For this reason, you should be very careful when placing portals, and don't place them too close to your home. It's also a good idea to build a fenced-off area around the portal, to stop any mobs from wandering into the overworld.

Portal travel

As well as your only conduit to the Nether, these portals also have another use – fast travel. In Minecraft, although the Nether is smaller in scale then the overworld, the two are still tied together, and match up after a scale reduction. This means that one block of movement in the Nether equals eight blocks in the overworld. This fact lets you exploit portals to travel great distances in the overworld. By building a portal to the Nether, travelling a distance in the hellish world and building a portal back, you can cover vast distances in the overworld in a fraction of the time it would usually take.

Exit portals will always be built in relative locations, and the game will try to match up the coordinates as best it can. This does mean that portals can be spawned in odd locations, but they should never appear in deadly areas like underwater.

Keep in mind that if a new portal is generated within 1024 blocks of an existing portal, both will link to the same location. This can be a little disorienting, so it's best to spread portals out a bit to keep your inter-dimensional travel straight.

Safe passage

Of course, if you do decide to use the Nether for fast travel, which is a good idea, as it's one of the most efficient ways to traverse the mammoth landscape, you'll have to brave the pitfalls and perils of the Nether, which isn't all

Fill this with Lava, and then pour water over one of the scaffolding blocks next to the lava so it flows over it. This will create obsidian again. Once again, drain the water

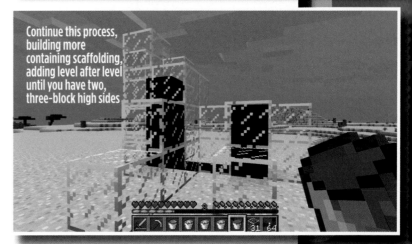

Continue this process, building more containing scaffolding, adding level after level until you have two, three-block high sides

At the top, use more blocks to create a four block trench on the top of the portal, and into this pour four buckets of lava, one for each block. Pour water onto a surrounding block and it'll wash over and cast the top of the portal. You're nearly done

Now mine away the scaffolding and use a flint and steel to ignite the portal and activate it. You've now got a working portal to the Nether, all without a single diamond or having to mine a single block of obsidian.

Mobs can also use Nether portals, such as these zombie pigmen

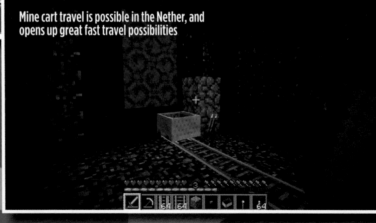

Mine cart travel is possible in the Nether, and opens up great fast travel possibilities

that desirable if you just want to get from A to B.

A good plan to make things better is to build your own Nether railway. By using mine cart tracks you can create your own Nether rail road, and if you want to ensure the safest possible journey, you can even encase the rail road within a well lit tunnel, helping to keep any nasties out.

Obviously, building in the Nether can be very, very tricky, but it's possible, and how cool is having your very own hellish ghost train?!

The Nether is a dangerous place, so you may want to spend time building an enclosed tunnel for your railway

10 ESSENTIAL TIPS FOR INTERMEDIATE PLAYERS

1 Building Bridges

If you want to get ahead in *Minecraft*, traversing large gaps with nothing but a steady-hand is a skill you'll need to develop. When you're holding the "sneak" button ([shift] on the PC version) you won't fall off ledges, and you can use this to create bridges by hanging as far over a gap as the game will let you and placing a block virtually under your own feet, allowing you to move another block forward. It's precarious, but it works a treat.

Just one example of the impressive, dynamic structures you can create using the Bridge Building technique!

2 Grow a Full-Size Jungle Tree

Once you've explored a Jungle biome, you'll probably wonder whether there's any way to make those giant trees grow anywhere else. There is: simply place four jungle saplings together in a square. When they grow they'll become a tree with a thick trunk and vines for climbing.

Four Jungle saplings. No good to anyone

Jungle Sapling

Save the planet by adding one mega-tree at a time

3 Barbecue Source

When you're on the lookout for animals to hunt and cook, did you know you can cut out the middle man by killing animals with fire? A Flint & Steel works best for this. That way, instead of dropping raw meat, they'll drop cooked stuff (i.e. cooked porkchop) which will give you back more health and allow you to get hot food without returning to a furnace and waiting for it to cook.

4 Diamond Mine

Finding Diamonds is essential for advancing your game, if only because they make the most durable tools, allowing you to focus on loftier pursuits. The best way to find diamonds is to mine a staircase down to the bedrock, then turn around, walk back up 11 blocks, then carve a 2 x 1 passage in a single direction. This is where diamonds appear most frequently!

5 Destroy Unwanted Blocks

If you've been digging mineshafts and are carrying a lot of blocks, you can get rid of them permanently. This is most easily accomplished by throwing them at fires, into lava, or (less obviously) at a cactus. It looks much tidier than leaving them strewn around the landscape, but it prevents you from picking the blocks up again, leaving your inventory empty for more important items.

6 Hook, Line and Sinker

If you've got an animal, mob or NPC that you want to corral in a specific direction then don't nudge them one block at a time. Instead, you can use a fishing rod to drag them around. Just cast as normal and make sure the hook lands on them, and you'll be able to pull them wherever it is you want to take them. To release them, simple switch from the rod or reel it in as normal!

7 Surfacing for Air

If you're near the bottom of the sea and running out of air, place a boat on the ground. It'll automatically start to rise to the surface, faster than you can swim, but slowly enough that you'll have time to get into it. You should reach the surface before your health runs out.

8 Hop, Sprint, Jump

By default you can move over land at three different speeds: sneaking, walking and sprinting. However, if you sprint and then repeatedly jump, this is slightly quicker than sprinting alone is.

Check your recipe book for accurate cooking times

9 Mind the Gap

When you're sprinting you might not realise that you can automatically step over 1-block gaps. Use this information to plan your routes and escape mobs quickly, although be careful – if you hit the gap at an angle you might fall in. Practise a few times!

10 Prepare to Dye

You probably know you can dye wools, but did you know you can dye sheep as well? Better yet, if you shear a dyed sheep, you'll get several blocks of coloured wool. This effectively triples the effectiveness of each unit of dye – if you shear a sheep then dye it, you need one unit per block of wool. Especially useful if you have some rare colours you want to use!

ADVANCED MINECRAFT TIPS & STRATEGIES

No time for chat - we've got a lot to get through this chapter! For this is where we unleash the more advanced ideas, tactics, strategies and secrets that can help turn a good *Minecraft* player into a great one! Hang around for the end of the chapter too, where we start to explore modding *Minecraft*: another element to the game's that's a whole lot of fun.

SURVIVING THE NETHER

Preparation

Before you go to the Nether you need to prepare, as it's not a very welcoming place. Taking the right supplies is paramount, although these supplies will vary depending on your goals in the alternate dimension.

Regardless of your reasons for travelling to the Nether, there are some things you simply must pack to increase your chances of survival, and these include a good sword, a bow and plenty of arrows. There are many dangerous enemies in the Nether, and you'll need to defend yourself. Many of these, such as the flying Ghast, require ranged attacks, so plenty of arrows are a must.

Always take a stack of torches. Despite being covered in lava, the Nether can be surprisingly dark, and without your own light sources, it can be tricky to navigate. Always have one or two stacks of torches to light your way.

The Nether is also very confusing, being a mass of maze-like tunnels, cliffs, and strongholds. Torches are also very useful as breadcrumb-style trails to lead you back to the portal.

As the Nether is dangerous, it's often a good idea to take some armour. However, as we stated in the early crafting guide, it's not a good idea to take precious armour like diamond, as it's easy to lose. The best overall armour is iron. It's affordable, and is the second most effective armour you can craft.

The environment in the Nether is fiery to say the least, with massive lakes of lava, lava flows and enemies that hurl fireballs at you. For this reason, a few potions of fire resistance are very useful, and greatly increase your chances of success. This applies especially if you're hunting Blazes. However, you need Nether wart to brew potions and a Blaze rod to make a potion stand, so a very careful trip or two is needed to the Nether first. If you're lucky, you may encounter a witch in the overworld who can sometimes drop fire resistance potions, so this may be worth a shot before venturing to the Nether.

Snowballs are another highly recommended item for Blaze hunting. They're an excellent weapon against the mob, and

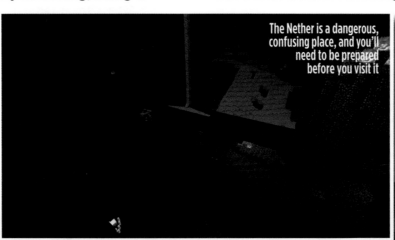

The Nether is a dangerous, confusing place, and you'll need to be prepared before you visit it

You can get stranded easily in the Nether, so bring materials to make an emergency portal

are plentiful, saving on harder to craft arrows.

You'll probably take quite a bit of damage and food is always needed, so you can stay full and regenerate health. Bring a packed lunch.

Occasionally, a Nether portal may appear on a floating island, or equally difficult place to get down from (even over lava). This can be a pain, but if you bring a couple of stacks of cobblestone, you should be able to build a bridge to somewhere more stable. Sand and/ or gravel is also useful, as gravity causes it to drop, making it easier to build a way down from a high portal spawn.

As it's so easy to get lost in the Nether, it can be a very good idea to bring another portal worth of obsidian, along with a flint and steel. This means that, if you're in the worst case scenario and can't get back to your entrance portal, you can at least build a new one back to the overworld.

Leave it at home

As the Nether is so dangerous, even a well-equipped and experienced player can meet and untimely demise. And, as much of this dying may involve lava, taking precious items you don't need to the Nether is a silly mistake to make.

Always leave behind your most valuable equipment, including diamond tools. There's nothing in the nether that can't be mined by iron, and Netherrack, which makes up much of the Nether, is one of the softest blocks in the game. Don't risk losing your best gear when you don't even need it.

A diamond sword can be handy in a fight, but again, it's risky. An iron sword is good enough, complemented with arrows. If you're confident in your abilities, though, the sword is the only diamond item you should risk, due to its usefulness.

Protect the portal

Arriving in the Nether is always a risky business. You never know where a portal will drop you, and what will be lurking in the immediate vicinity. Once you arrive, and if the portal you're using is exposed, it's a very good idea to protect the area around the portal. Whilst the frame is obsidian, and so very hardy, the portal can still be disabled by a rogue Ghast fireball (you can re-ignite it, though), and the ground around the portal can be destroyed, making it hard to reach. This isn't good if you're in trouble and need to leave quickly. It's also worth noting that another Ghast fireball hit may reactivate a portal too, so you can try to fool a Ghast into doing this for you if needs be.

To help make your possible

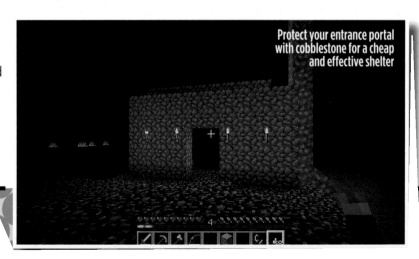

Protect your entrance portal with cobblestone for a cheap and effective shelter

fast retreats, build a protective shell around your portal area. Use cobblestone or more durable blocks to ensure Ghast fireballs don't do any damage as Netherrack is very weak.

With your shelter built, you may want to set up a base camp, complete with crafting table and furnace, so you can craft supplies if you need to without going back to the overworld.

out the burning with some health left. Golden apples, thanks to their increased regeneration, may also prevent an early death. Travelling through the Nether portal will put you out too, although this may not be of much help if you're a distance from it. At the very least, do your best to get to a relatively safe area so your items drop in a location where you can retrieve them.

Fire swimming

Potions of fire resistance and enchanted golden apples don't just protect you from fire-based attacks, but also from lava. In fact, with their effects active, you can actually swim through lava, which is a very handy skill to have in the Nether. Just be sure to keep checking that timer, and don't get stuck in the lava when it ticks down.

Baby steps

On your first trip to the Nether, you'll probably have no real goals, such as finding Blaze rods or harvesting Nether wart, you'll just want to explore the hellish dimension. At first, don't stray too far from the portal, instead simply get a feel for the Nether. At any point you can hit lava, a dangerous foe, or drop off a cliff you didn't see due to low light. With experience, you'll learn the

Burn, baby, burn

Buckets of water are staple items for miners wishing to avoid a hot, fiery death in the overworld, but this isn't so in the Nether. Water cannot be created in the Nether, as it evaporates too quickly. So, pouring a bucket over yourself isn't really possible. So, if you're on fire, you could be in a lot of trouble.

Fire resistance potions can help greatly, as we've already mentioned, and if you're on lower difficulties, you may actually be able to wait

pitfalls and how to survive, and you'll be able to make longer excursions into the world.

Nether mining

As Netherrack is very soft and easy to mine, you can quickly dig your way through the Nether with almost any tool. This means you can amass a large amount of Netherrack quickly, which can be useful as a building material.

Be careful, though, a Netherrack is easily set on fire, and will burn forever, or until it's put out or destroyed. This can be a useful trait however,

The Nether is largely made up of flimsy and flammable Netherrack

and Netherrack can not only be useful when creating mob traps such as fire pits, but it can also be useful for decorative effects like fireplaces.

As it's easy to mine through, you can get carried away digging tunnels at speed, but you should be careful. You can easily dig into an unseen lava lake, or even stumble upon hidden lava source blocks. As with mining in the overworld, always be vigilant, especially as you have no water on hand.

Another useful resource you can find in the Nether is Soul Sand. This is a strange block that causes whatever passes over it to slow down, much like quick sand. It's also the only block you can use to grow Nether Wart when you have it. It's easy to mine, and you can find it all over the Nether. It's ability to slow down enemies makes it a great block to use for home defence, and surrounding your base with it can help make attackers easier to deal with.

Aside from lava, the only other real source of light in the Nether comes from Glowstones, which can usually be seen growing from ceilings in the realm. When mined, these blocks drop several piles of Glowstone dust, which you can use to make your own Glowstone blocks. Glowstone dust is also used to craft firework stars, and in potion brewing. As Glowstone blocks often spawn high up on ceilings, they can be hard to reach without building up to them. You can do this easily enough by jump-building a pillar of blocks up to a cluster of Glowstones, but ensure there are no foes, especially the deadly Ghasts, nearby when you do. If you're lucky, you may find a growth of Glowstones on a low ceiling or in a tunnel.

Nether Quartz is also spread around the world, and this is used to create Quartz items. It's easy enough to mine, and should cause no real problems.

Glowstones can be hard to reach, but are worth it for many reasons

Nether fortresses

Just as in the overworld, you can find strongholds in the Nether, instead called fortresses. In fact, due to the smaller scale of the alternate realm compared to the overworld, it's easier to find these structures, and it's here where most of your Nether-side goals will be found.

One of the most dangerous finds in Nether fortresses are monster spawners spitting out Blazes. Blazes are a very dangerous enemy for the ill-prepared, but they're also the only way to get Blaze rods, so if you want to brew potions (the brewing stand needs a Blaze rod, and rods can also be turned in Blaze powder, needed for Ender Pearls) you'll need to fight blazes. If you do this, bring snowballs and some golden apples, as you won't have potions unless you've picked them up from a witch. Enchanted

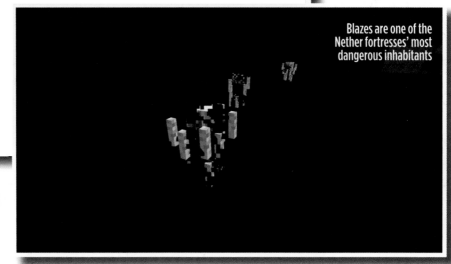

Blazes are one of the Nether fortresses' most dangerous inhabitants

Fortresses in the Nether are home to important enemies and items, such as Blazes, Wither skeletons, Nether wart and so on. They're also a very good source of Nether brick, which can be mined and taken. They're dangerous places, but lucrative ones. Nether fortresses are also very dark, with limited light sources, so you'll need to ensure you place plenty of torches. They can be complex structures, and it's very easy to come a cropper thanks to an unseen drop.

golden apples will even grant you five minutes of fire resistance, perfect for fighting Blazes.

Snow golems use snowballs as their attack, and so can theoretically be a danger to Blazes, but they also take constant damage due to the Nether's heat, so they're not that useful unless you make a load of them.

Iron golems, on the other hand, can be very helpful, so creating one and leashing it, then taking it into action can be a great idea.

The difficult part of attacking a Blaze spawner is actually getting to the spawner, as Blazes spawn constantly. Pushing forward can be tricky, but it is possible with enough patience. The problem is, once the spawner is gone, no more Blazes will spawn, and so you'll have no more source of Blaze rods. So, a good idea is to kill a few Blazes and then leave the spawner.

Nether mob drops

Just as Blazes drop Blaze rods, which are essential for potion brewing, other Nether mobs drop valuable and rare items too, many of which are also used for brewing potions.

Ghasts, which drop Ghast tears, are one of the most difficult mobs to harvest, not only as they're dangerous, but also as they usually fly around, often over lava. So, if you kill one, it's very possible to lose the drop as it falls into the lava. When fighting Ghasts, always try to kill them over land so you can grab the Ghast tear and gunpowder they drop. A fishing rod can be useful for this, as you can catch and reel in a Ghast.

Obviously, this is very risky, but it means you can control where you kill them. And remember, you can hit Ghast fireballs back at them too.

Zombie pigmen are a very tough foe when enraged, and it's often best to leave them be. However, they can also drop gold nuggets, rotten flesh, and rarely gold ingots and golden swords, so taking the risk can be worthwhile. If you do intend to attack a zombie pigman or two, try to make sure they're separated from a group, as the last thing you need is a gaggle of these zombified foes attacking you at once. Ranged attacks are preferable here.

Magma cubes are the only natural source of Magma Cream (it can also be man-made using Blaze powder and a Slimeball). This is key to brewing fire resistance potions. So, if you want to become fire proof, kill a few Magma cubes.

Wither Skeletons are tough, tall skeletons that spawn in Nether fortresses. When killed they drop coal and bones, and rarely stone swords and Wither skeleton skulls. The latter of these objects is used to summon the Wither boss, and you'll need three to do so.

Ghasts are troublesome foes, arguably more so due to their movement than their attack

ENCHANTMENTS

Enchanting your items is both a fun way of improving your cherished gear and an essential part of tackling the game's bigger challenges. How do you expect to survive a foray into the Nether without enchanted armour and weapons for taking on those tougher mobs?

Fortunately enchanting is relatively easy to get started with, at least compared with potion-brewing. All you need to get started is obsidian, a little diamond and a book (and if you don't know how to craft a book, may I gently suggest you skip back a few pages before tackling enchantment!).

Once you've crafted an Enchantment Table using those items, you'll also need experience points to invest in your enchantments. Fortunately by the time you're ready to begin enchanting you'll probably have quite a few levels to spare.

Enchantment Basics

When you first activate your Enchantment Table you'll be confronted with a set of empty slots. Your first step should be selecting an item you want to enchant and placing it on the table. At this point you'll see a set of three options appear, each marked with a set of mysterious runes and a green number.

Here's some *Minecraft* trivia for you: those runes are entirely meaningless, and are in fact randomly generated from a pool of words! What really matters are the green numbers, and what really, really matters is how large they are. They relate to the number of experience levels you can invest in an enchantment, and the higher the number the more powerful your enchantment is likely to turn out.

It's impossible to specify particular enchantments using an Enchantment Table, so be prepared to try a few times to find the specific enchantment you're after.

Enchantment Tables absorb mystic power from the libraries around them

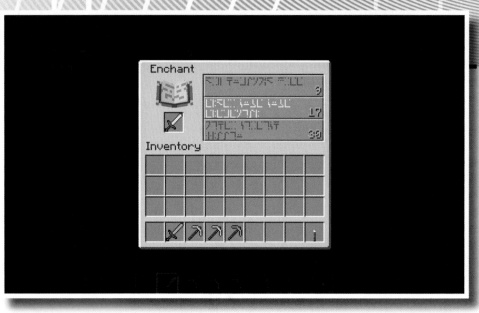

Getting the Best Out of Enchanting

There are two considerations for enchanting: the first are the experience levels you're able to invest; and the second relates to the number of bookshelves you have near your Enchantment Table.

Experience is gained during play from activities such as mining rare ore (even coal!) and killing monsters. Chances are that by the time you're able to begin enchanting you've got a few levels to play with – unless you've been unlucky enough to get yourself killed, which can involve major loss of experience levels.

You do retain some experience after death, and if you can find where you died you can collect some of the lost orbs alongside your dropped equipment. It's not uncommon for players to lose 50% or more of their collected experience upon death, however, so the best advice possible is: don't die!

Bookshelves are crafted from wooden planks and books and are fairly easy to craft in large numbers once you've gotten basic wood and sugar cane farming under your belt. This is fortunate as you'll need quite a few bookshelves to maximise your enchantment efficiency: up to fifteen in all, with each increasing the maximum possible level of enchantment available.

The Mechanics of Enchanting

The maximum experience level that it's possible to invest at an Enchantment Table is 30. It's important to note that the experience level spent at an Enchantment Table doesn't directly relate to the types of enchantment that can result: it just increases the probability of getting the best enchantments.

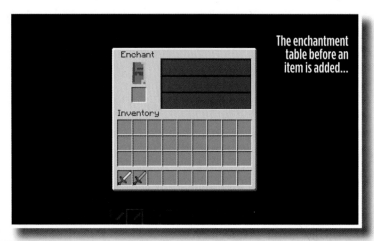

The enchantment table before an item is added...

Enchantments themselves are distinguished in levels marked with Roman Numerals, from I to V, with some items not permitting enchantments above III or IV.

The layout of bookshelves around an Enchantment Table also matters: the space between the bookshelves and the table needs to be uninterrupted. Carpets, snow, torches etc will all count as

Enchantments for Tools

Most enchantments can be applied to any tool but let's be honest: who wants a magical spade anyway? Efficiency is the most common enchantment for tools and it increases your mining/harvesting speed by 30% each level. These effects stack, so Efficiency V is almost three times as fast at Efficiency I.

Unbreaking increases durability which helps any item last longer: obviously useful, but not that sexy. Fortune is more exciting, as it applies a stacking percentage chance each level to increase the number of resources that drop from each block or resource. Fortune is so useful that some players recommend not mining emeralds, diamonds and other rare resources until you have a pick with this enchantment!

The holy grail of tool enchantments is Silk Touch, which allows you to collect many blocks that are otherwise unobtainable. Okay, it may not sound that useful, but it's rare, and when you're playing *Minecraft* at an extremely high level, sometimes you want to be able to harvest unique blocks to decorate your replica of Minas Tirith (or whatever floats your boat). You can also enchant your fishing rod. Luck of the Sea will increase the chance of catching a 'treasure' item and decrease the chance of 'junk' catches. Lure is the better enchantment, as it makes fish bite your hook five seconds faster per level as well as applying a similar effect to Luck of the Sea, making fishing more efficient overall.

The sheer, unbridled power!

Repair & Name
Diamond Sword
Enchantment Cost 8

'blocking' bookshelves off from the Enchantment Table. Note that you can take advantage of this curious effect to limit the effectiveness of your library: if you want to enchant an item using lower experience levels, just place some torches and try the Enchantment Table again.

The enchantments available are also randomised, so if you don't like what's presented to you when you place an item on the Enchantment Table, just back out and try it again until the experience levels you can spend are what you're after.

The top slot in the enchantment table represents the lowest range of enchantment, and the bottom the highest. With fifteen

bookshelves around your table the bottom slot will always allow 30 levels; at the other end of the scale, with no bookshelves at all the top slot will allow only 1 or 2. There's a lot of variation between the various experience levels you can spend, so do take your time.

Sadly there's no way to exert any control over the actual enchantments you'll get. Certain enchantments are more likely than others and it's down to the roll of the dice what you'll end up with. However, the more experience levels you invest, the higher the chances of getting a second, third or even a fourth enchantment alongside the first!

Enchantments for Weapon & Armour

Weapons and Armour have the largest range of enchantments available, with eight available for armour, six for swords and four for bows. We'd recommend applying enchantments only to your best equipment! The most common armour enchantment is Protection which reduces damage from most sources, so you're guaranteed something fairly useful no matter what happens. Feather Fall reduces damage from falling, which is very useful when exploring caves. Fire, Projectile and the less common Blast Protection are all fairly obvious in their effects, though Blast Protection also reduces knockback from explosions.

Respiration and Aqua Affinity are useful underwater, helping you to breath for longer and see better, and mine underwater at a faster rate respectively. They're almost as rare as Thorns, which inflicts damage on anything attacking you – although it can also accelerate the rate at which your armour degrades.

For swords, the common effect Sharpness increases damage against all enemies, whilst Smite adds a more generous bonus against skeletons, zombies and other undead creatures and Bane of Arthropods does the same for spiders (and, fact fans, silverfish). Note that these three enchantments can also be applied to axes.

Knockback is another obvious enchantment: if you like to wallop monsters off cliffs, it's pretty good fun. Fire Aspect is similarly entertaining as it sets anything attacked alight. You can even attack animals and have them drop cooked meat. Finally, Looting means that defeated creatures are more likely to drop good loot.

Last but not least: the humble bow. The first three enchantments available are very like their sword equivalents: Power increases damage, Punch increases Knockback and Flame sets targets on fire. The rarest enchantment, Infinity, allows you to shoot your bow without using up arrows. All you need is to have one arrow!

Advanced Enchanting

The most advanced form of enchanting is applying multiple enchantments to a single item. As noted above it's possible to receive multiple enchantments on an item at an Enchantment Table, but this is uncommon and can't be relied upon to acquire specific enchantments.

You can however enchant books, and books have the unique property of being able to receive any enchantment – that is to say, enchantments that only have any effect when applied to weapons, tools or armour. It's then possible to combine enchanted books with other items, essentially applying the book's enchantment to another item, even if that item already has its own enchantments. In this way you can power up items with two, , five or even ten enchantments.

Don't try to apply multiple enchantments to individual books – it won't work as books may only have a single enchantment each! In order to combine enchanted books with your weapons, tools and armour, you'll need an anvil. Anvils aren't hard to come by; you just need a lot of iron: 31 iron ingots. 27 of those will need to be formed into solid iron blocks, and the remaining four form the anvil's stand. Once you've accomplished that just place the item you wish to enchant in this first slot and the book in the second.

You can also combine levels of enchantments in this way. A book with Sharpness I applied to an Iron Sword with Sharpness I will produce an Iron Sword with Sharpness II! Similarly you can 'pool' their enchantments into a single item, although this will destroy the second item forever.

OTIONS

The ancient art of alchemy may be best known for the legend of transmuting lead into gold, but in *Minecraft* the focus is on brewing up potions. Some can heal, some can harm and others provide a variety of temporary status effects, enabling players to survive dangers or traverse areas they'd otherwise steer clear of. Potion-brewing is still a major area of development at Mojang, so don't be surprised if through experimentation you find new recipes down the line. In fact, we encourage experimentation with your brewing – that's the fun! The other half is sampling your own wares (but take care not to drink anything poisonous).

Getting Started

As with Enchanting, Potion brewing only really becomes an option once you've gained the ability to acquire diamond and obsidian. Unlike Enchanting, Potion brewing also requires you to have travelled to the Nether. Building a Brewing Stand requires a Blaze Rod, which you can only acquire by defeating a Blaze in the Nether.

You'll also need some glass bottles, but I think we can safely agree that smelting glass and making bottles is a fair bit simpler than creating an intra-dimensional hell portal.

If you're struggling to find a Blaze, well... you're not going to like this, but you need to look inside a Nether Fortress. They will either spawn naturally there, or you'll encounter up to four at any time from a Blaze monster spawner. They're dangerous enemies, found only in dangerous places, so it's safe to say that Potion brewing is something that you should only set out to do when you feel you're ready.

Enchantments can make traversing the Nether and exploring fortresses a lot safer, so do check out our guide to enchanting your items if you need a leg up. Once you've got your precious blaze rod safely back to base, you'll be pleased to hear that all you need to complete the Brewing Stand crafting recipe is three blocks of cobblestone. Phew!

Although cauldrons – which were used for potion-brewing in earlier versions of *Minecraft* – are no longer an essential component, they are still useful for filling water bottles. Dump a bucket of water in a cauldron and you've enough water for three glass bottles. Now you're thinking with alchemy!

I've always been partial to a spot of open-air brewing

Finding Potion Ingredients

Potions start with one of four ingredients: Nether Wart, Fermented Spider Eye, Glowstone dust, or Redstone. Of these, Nether Wart leads to the exciting potions: the others lead to different types of Potion of Weakness.

Nether Wart is a plant found only in the Nether, of course, and can generally be found in Nether Fortresses around staircases (or, if you're playing on the Xbox version, on soul sand beaches). Best keep an eye out for some Nether Wart whilst you're hunting down your first blaze rod!

Nether Warts can be farmed, though you'll also need to bring some soul sand back with you to accomplish this. Nether Wart seeds should be planted on soul sand, and then it's just a matter of waiting for the plant to grow through four stages. Bone meal and light levels have no effect on Nether Wart, so feel free to grow it alongside mushrooms underground.

Note that the second and third stages look the same, so the best way to judge if it's ready is to see whether the plant looks darker than it did, and if the stalks have no gaps between them.

In addition to the ingredients I've already mentioned, different potions can also be produced through combinations of blaze powder, magma cream, regular (non-fermented) spider eye, glistening melons, ghast tears, sugar, pufferfish and golden carrots.

Redstone and sugar are very common ingredients; by the time you're brewing potions you should have plenty of both, or at least know where to find some. Glistening melons and golden carrots are both acquired by crafting a regular melon or carrot with gold nuggets, which is a little trickier but by this stage of the game not much of a challenge.

Spider eyes are also fairly commonplace as they are dropped by spiders, cave spiders and witches upon death. To get the fermented variety, just add sugar and a brown mushroom. It may surprise you to hear but fermented spider-eyes are entirely inedible as opposed to normal spider eyes, which are delicious enough to eat even though they're poisonous. Pufferfish are similarly bad for you but are harder to find – you may find yourself fishing for a long time before you land one.

Blaze powder can only be acquired by breaking down blaze rods (hope you saved a spare). Ghast tears and Magma cream are also monster drops. Tears are tricky to get thanks to the fondness Ghasts have for floating over inaccessible areas. Still, no one said brewing would be easy! Magma cream is easier to come by – Magma Cubes split into smaller versions of themselves much as Slimes do, and all large or medium-sized Magma Cubes have a chance to drop precious cream upon death.

The final ingredient, glowstone dust, is also a product of the Nether. Unusually for the Nether it doesn't involve having to kill anything unpleasant and dangerous at all: it's easily found by mining glowstone blocks.

You can't hurl potions far, but they hit hard

Starter Recipes

This section concerns potions involving just one or two ingredients that are relatively easy to come by. We recommend that everyone brewing for the first time tries these simple recipes to get the hang of the process. The last thing you want is to accidentally waste an extremely precious Ghast tear!

When you open your Brewing Stand you'll immediately see that there are slots for three bottles with one ingredient above. You can apply one ingredient to three potions simultaneously – which means you can potentially use rare ingredients efficiently to create multiple potions.

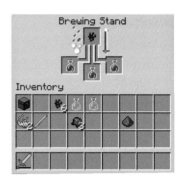

Potions of weakness are the potions you'll most often end up with through pure experimentation, and they're of limited usefulness. All they do is reduce melee damage by 50%. You won't want to drink them yourself, although they can be useful as Splash Potions (see Advanced Recipes on the next page).

Adding Glowstone dust followed by a Fermented Spider Eye, Nether Wart followed by a Fermented Spider Eye, or Fermented Spider Eye on its own will produce a potion of weakness that lasts for a minute and a half. In the unlikely event that you do want a potion of weakness, just use the Fermented Spider Eye on its own.

You can produce a longer-lasting Potion of Weakness by using Redstone followed by a Fermented Spider Eye – this variant will last for a more substantial four minutes, although it's unlikely that you'll be fighting many creatures that take so long to defeat!

Useful potions that are relatively easy to make all start with Nether Wart, as do most of the advanced recipes we've included

for you, so do try and stock up on this vital ingredient. To create a simple Potion of Healing, first add Nether Wart and then add a Glistening Melon. The resulting potion will instantly restore two hearts of health.

A Potion of Swiftness can be created by adding Nether Wart followed by Sugar. This potion is handy for escaping a tight spot as it increases your speed by 20%, which stacks with sprinting, allowing you to cover more ground. It lasts for three minutes which should be enough time to make your escape.

Nether Wart followed by Golden Carrot produces a rather useful Potion of Night Vision, which for three minutes will light your darkest hours. If you accidentally find yourself stranded somewhere dangerous at night, this could mean the difference between life and death.

Finally, you can produce a Potion of Poison by adding Nether Wart and Spider Eye. This lasts for 45 seconds and will deal up to eighteen hearts of damage. As with the Potion of Weakness, it's not something you'll want to drink yourself, but as a Splash Potion it can be useful against powerful enemies.

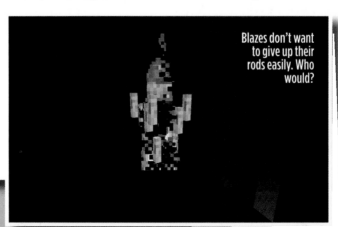

Blazes don't want to give up their rods easily. Who would?

Advanced Recipes

Below you'll find a few more recipes to get you brewing, but first it's important to understand the principles of the 'modifier' ingredients: Redstone, Glowstone dust and Fermented Spider Eye.

In the previous section we saw that these ingredients by themselves typically produced useless potions, or Potions of Weakness. However, they actually have properties that no other ingredients do when applied to an existing potion.

Redstone makes a potion last longer. Add it to your Potion of Night Vision or your Potion of Swiftness for impressive results.

Glowstone dust makes a potion more potent – although it usually also makes a potion's effects last for less time. Still, try adding it to a Potion of Healing – you'll find that your potion now heals four hearts of health instead of two.

Fermented Spider Eye is a more risky proposition, as it often inverts the effects of a potion. For example, add it to a Potion of Strength and you're left with another Potion of Weakness. But add it to a Potion of Night Vision and you'll end up with something very different, but still very useful...

The following potions all begin with Nether Wart. Adding Pufferfish gets you a Potion of Water Breathing. Blaze Powder gets you a Potion of Strength. Magma Cream results in a Potion of Fire Resistance, and Ghast Tear results in a Potion of Regeneration. All of these potions can be enhanced with the modifier ingredients I just mentioned – so experiment!

The final trick to remember is that you can add Gunpowder to any potion in order to make it a Splash Potion. What's a Splash Potion? It's a potion you can throw! At last, you can get your own back on Creepers by using their own drops against them.

Potions of Swiftness: for the fastest getaway!

A potion of healing can be handy if friendly villagers are hurt

5 UNEXPECTED USES FOR A BUCKET OF WATER

Extinguish Fires

Things catching fire can be a huge problem, especially if that thing is you. A bucket of water can be used to instantly extinguish fires in locations where you'd otherwise be unable to, whether they're caused by lightning, lava or a mob's misplaced fireball. If you fall into lava, you can even use it to protect yourself. Dropping a bucket of water will transform lava into obsidian or cobblestone, allowing you to pull yourself to safety.

Defend Yourself!

Flowing water doesn't affect solid blocks, but it'll push back almost anything else it comes into contact with: items, mined resources, players, NPCs and even mobs. If you find yourself backed into a corner, you might be able to use a water flow to slow down your enemies or keep them at bay entirely. And, of course, Endermen are hurt by water, making buckets a useful defensive tool for keeping them at a distance.

Long grass can be irritating to get rid of...

Clear The Area

Some placed items will pop when they come into contact with flowing water – crops, flowers, long grass, torches and rails, for example. If you ever want to quickly collect or remove these items from an area, it's far easier to drop a single water block and let the resulting spring wipe the ground clean than it is to break them all individually!

Creating More Water

If you've got two blocks of water, you can create an infinite source by digging a small pit (4x4 is best) and placing two blocks of water diagonally opposite one another. This will create a self-replenishing well – as soon as you pick up one water block, it'll be instantly refilled by the blocks next to it! Particularly useful if you're underground or atop a tower and need extra water.

Water, water, everywhere, but sadly no requirement to drink

5 UNEXPECTED USES FOR A BUCKET OF LAVA

f you thought a bucket of water was a handy accessory, you'll be amazed by what can be accomplished with a bucket of lava. Truly, it is the Swiss Army Knife of bucket-fluid combinations...

Harness Geothermal Power

A bucket of Lava makes an excellent fuel for smelting – it lasts longer than coal and is about as easy to come by if you've got a bucket handy. A single piece of coal will burn for 80 seconds, smelting a maximum of 8 items. A bucket of lava, by comparison, burns for 1000 seconds and can smelt 100 items.

Fight Monsters

Lava doesn't just harm players – few mobs can withstand it either. As long as you can avoid its flow, placing lava during a fight might help you finish your enemies before they get anywhere near you, and at very little personal risk. Beware, though – if your foes drop any items when they die, there's a good chance they'll be incinerated!

Light The Way

Lava makes an excellent (if potentially destructive) source of light, emitting the maximum light level of 15 units (Torches emit 14 units, Redstone ore emits 9 units when touched). Relying on it exclusively would be inefficient, given how easy it is to make torches, but if you find yourself running out of wood or simply want to make an impressive-looking light feature in your base then lava will do the trick. In arctic biomes, lava can also be used to melt snow and ice!

Let's all bathe in this lava's warm, glowing, warming glow

Farm Blocks

Lava and water can be combined to create a number of blocks. When lava flows onto still water, it creates Stone. When water flows onto flowing lava, it creates cobblestone. And when water flows onto still lava, it creates the mystical Obsidian.

Start Fires

Minecraft allows you to safely explore pyromania, and lava makes an excellent way to begin one because unlike traditional sources of fire, it can ignite multiple blocks quickly. A lava flow is a good way to burn out a forest, bring down structures and incinerate cobwebs. Of course, uncontrolled Lava itself isn't particularly easy to get rid of in its own right, but take care and a lava-fuelled inferno will eliminate those blocks for you.

5 UNEXPECTED USES FOR A TORCH

The humble torch is one of *Minecraft*'s most sought-after items, if only for its ability to illuminate dark corners and stave ⬚ mobs. But did you know there are some other ways you can use it to⬚

Build On A Torch

Torches count as blocks in their own right, so you can actually place blocks adjacent to a torch even if that'd leave it handing in mid-air. This is especially useful for creating staircases up towards ceilings and high-up areas, because torches are quicker to pick up and navigate around than other temporary blocks would be.

Light the Way

A good technique to keep your bearings is to maintain a system using your torches – for example, you might always place torches on the left side of the cave passage while exploring. That way, you'll be able to follow them back to the entrance more easily by making sure the torches stay on your right. If they're on your left, you know you've gotten turned around and that you're going in circles!

Torches lighting the way, like a trail of breadcrumbs would if they were on fire

Automatically Harvest Sand & Gravel

Rather than digging piles of sand out by hand, you can use a torch to automatically harvest the blocks as they fall. Place a torch in the space below whatever the sand is resting on, then mine that block. The sand will fall, but instead of piling up on top, it'll instantly pop, allowing you to collect (or discard) it at will. Much easier than waiting for each block it to settle before you dig it, and it works the same for gravel.

Taking a Breath

While underwater, placing a torch will create a small air pocket that can be used to replenish your breath. The water will cause the torch to pop immediately, but it doesn't matter – you can pick it up straight away and one gasp of air is more than enough to fill your lungs.

Celebrate Halloween

Combining a torch with a Pumpkin creates a spooky-looking Jack O' Lantern. Fun, yes, but why would you want waste a valuable torch on suc frivolity? Well, Jack O' Lanter are slightly more luminous tha torches. Like Lava, they have a light value of 15, whereas torches have just 14. They can even emit light underwater!

5 UNEXPECTED USES FOR GRAVEL

At first glance, gravel is the most useless block in the game with no obvious practical application. When mined it has a 10% chance of turning into flint, but the abundance of gravel means you'll quickly find yourself with more flint than you'll ever need.

But gravel isn't all bad. It's one of only two naturally-occurring blocks in the game that obey gravity, and the other – sand – has more obvious value because it can be smelted into glass, crafted into sandstone and mixed with gunpowder to create TNT. So what can you use gravel for?

Traps

Falling blocks can injure, even kill a player or mob. One of the simplest traps in *Minecraft* uses this fact to its advantage. By using pistons and pressure pads, you can set up a simple redstone system that pushes gravel blocks onto your enemies below, killing them. And if it leaves you with a mess, at least it's one that's easy to reset!

Staircases

Again, this application uses the fact that gravel responds to gravity to its advantage. If you've got a steep drop to get down but also need a quick way up, you can lean over the edge (hold the sneak button so you don't fall!) and place gravel adjacent to the block you're standing on. It'll fall to the bottom and begin to pile up. When the pillar is one block below you, drop down and start the process again. You'll quickly have a useful and simple staircase.

Pillars

You can use any block to build pillars beneath if you want to get up high, but gravel is especially good for two reasons: it can be mined quickly with a spade, so the pillar can be easily dismantled, and because it's affected by gravity you can also dismantle large pillars from the base.

This gravel pillar might look ugly, but it can be easily dismantled now its purpose has been served

Decoration!

Gravel isn't the prettiest block, but it does have some aesthetic value. If you're laying overground tracks for a minecart, placing gravel beneath the rails gives them an authentic real-world feel. It's the details that make Minecraft, and this one is a fantastic touch that'll improve your design considerably.

Filling in Lava Pits

Filling in a lava lake destroys the lava source blocks, getting rid of the threat for good. Dropping gravel into lava lakes is an ideal way to make sure the whole thing is filled in, because it allows you to fill up blocks you can't physically reach. You can also use the same technique to fill in lakes and deep pits!

WORLD GENERATION & FINDING THE RIGHT BIOME FOR YOU

Creating New Worlds

Minecraft doesn't offer a huge number of options when it comes to customising new worlds. Turning structures on and off, activating cheats, a bonus chest... these either sound like ways to make the game less fun or a crutch for new players.

Generating a world of the 'superflat' variety can be interesting; this generates a world that is just four layers deep. The default is one layer of bedrock, two of dirt, and one of grass, although there are other presets you can select.

Generally speaking, superflats exist for two purposes: firstly for players who are happy spending every waking hour fending off endlessly spawning slimes in survival mode, and secondly for players who want a blank canvas to play with in creative mode. The flat surfaces combined with infinite resources of every type means it's easy to quickly assemble vast, impressive structures or cities.

But for most players, and those of you reading this book, it's likely that Survival mode is what interests you. Fortunately *Minecraft* includes one option for you, and that's the use of 'seeds'.

Seeds are essentially strings of numbers or words that are fed into *Minecraft*'s world-builder algorithm (the calculation it performs to work out how a world will be generated). They work consistently when input into the same version of the *Minecraft* world-builder, so friends playing the same (or similar) versions of the game will be able to play independently in the same world.

Sadly seeds differ between the PC, Xbox and mobile versions of the game, and older seeds are less likely to work with newer versions of the game. For that reason we've only included a few here – they date quickly! The best place to get seeds is from friends or *Minecraft* communities.

PC seeds: [SG: these work in 1.7.4 – but may not work in March!]

20478739626 – starts you off next to an impressive Mesa biome that has appeared in a large canyon.

For some, a seed that starts you right next to a Jungle Temple is nothing short of perfection

Caught between rare mesa and common desert... nice, but where's the stone?

Somewhere with plenty of wood and stone is a decent start

-8797494547566195007 - there are lots of Extreme Hills nearby, a great source of the diamonds and other rare resources, as well as an NPC village and a forest.

Xbox 360 seeds: [SG: these are untested – I don't own the game on this platform!] 3634578730342032221 - starts you close to a blacksmith on a lake, with a nether portal nearby. There are plenty of other uncommon biomes nearby, including jungles.

-1763857877073745322 - another seed with nearby access to every biome you could desire, plus multiple abandoned mineshafts and villages.

Pocket Edition seeds: [SG: these are untested – I don't own the game on this platform!] -1184284029 - flat land to build on near a huge valley, with coal, iron and gold nearby too. LightShadows - a great seed for beginners or Creative mode, with lots of trees, bamboo and rolling hills.

Exploring Your World

Let's say you don't want to start in a particular biome – you just want to find those you need. This is unfortunately where it gets tricky.

Minecraft worlds handle biome placement using a 'temperature' system. For the Snowy biomes this is set at "under 0.15"; for Cold biomes it's between 0.2 and 0.3, Lush ranges all the way between 0.6 and 0.95, and many of the Dry biomes are "over 1.0" all the way up to 2.0.

The world generator places biomes next to one another based on temperature shifts – so

Some things never change: wherever you start, the first order of work is a shelter for the night!

that you don't end up with Ice Plains and a Desert right next to each other, for example. Unfortunately this means that rare biomes at uncommon temperature points – Ice Plains Spikes, Mesa and Jungles in particular – can only occur between specific other biomes, and at a reduced frequency.

Put simply, you're far more likely to find common biomes in the only places where rare biomes can occur. This is most true of the Mushroom Island biomes. You could search the ocean for days without stumbling across one.

Hope is not lost, however. Minecraft is ultimately a game all about exploration, and if you've got a compass to guide you back home (or don't mind dying and losing all your items – exploring with disposable equipment isn't a bad idea at all) then a trip in a certain direction can be a lot of fun. You can help ensure you're on the right track by, for example, following where the sun rises and sets.

If you're playing on PC, the modding community does have a few tricks up its sleeve to help you out. A utility called AMIDST directly accesses your Minecraft world files and identifies biomes, strongholds, villages, witch huts, temples – and the player's current location. This is invaluable as it can tell you, for example, that the closest Jungle biome is to the East – saving you a fruitless journey in any other direction that could have wasted hours.

For more on mods, check out the Modding pages in the Advanced section of this book.

For Xbox and mobile Minecrafters, I'm afraid you're stuck with the traditional approach. Explore your worlds, and try to follow the borders of biomes similar to the one you're looking for - or just strike out in whatever direction feels right to you!

REDSTONE CIRCUITS

Redstone can be used for many magnificent devices in Minecraft, and here are some tips to get you going

Powered by Redstone

As one of the most plentiful rare ores, Redstone is one of the most flexible materials not directly used for building. Rather than forming a sturdy wall, Redstone's power comes from its, er... power. Yes, Redstone dust conducts electricity and when paired with power providing items like Redstone torches and levers, you can use this magical dust to create complex circuits and machinery. It's a vital element of mine cart tracks, lighting, automatic doors and many other *Minecraft* devices. To use it, however, you need to posses some knowledge of circuitry.

Redstone power

Before you start to build circuits and devices, you need to know some of the core properties of Redstone dust. Firstly, Redstone dust, or wire, can generate a power level of up to 15, and this level drops one digit per block, meaning that a basic, unassisted Redstone dust trail can carry power for no more than 15 blocks. As it goes, the trail grows darker and darker to signify the loss of power.

This level can be increased or lowered by other devices attached to the trail. For example, daylight sensors can raise or lower the power level (depending on the amount of sunlight), whilst a Redstone repeater will output a level of 15 when turned on, extending the range of a single circuit.

Redstone wire will power any adjacent block of wire on the same level, or on a level one block higher or lower. However, this can be affected by block opacity. Most core building blocks in *Minecraft* are opaque, and these can power dust one level higher or lower. Transparent blocks such as glass, however, cannot power dust on lower levels, as you can't place Redstone onto them. The block above and next to

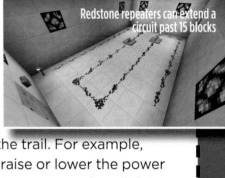
Redstone repeaters can extend a circuit past 15 blocks

Unassisted Redstone wire will only carry power for 15 blocks

Redstone wire can power adjacent blocks, but there are limits

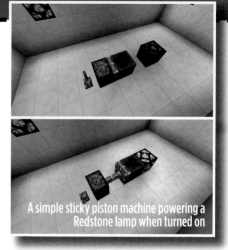

A simple sticky piston machine powering a Redstone lamp when turned on

functional devices, you can use sticky pistons to create moving machines, such as doors or floors. Redstone blocks make this very easy to do.

Core blocks

Aside from Redstone wire, there are many other core circuit blocks you'll need to use to construct devices. Other blocks such as doors and fence gates can also be used, but they're not limited to Redstone use. We'll talk about mine cart-specific blocks, such as powered rails, in the mine cart section of this guidebook.

Redstone torch

The most basic method of powering Redstone wire is a Redstone torch. These will power wire adjacent to them, and also blocks above and wire below it. This makes them very flexible for sending power both horizontally and vertically. For more on this, see 'Upstairs, Downstairs' below.

Redstone blocks

Unlike Redstone dust, blocks are already powered, and can power both blocks (like the Redstone lamp) and wire trails. They're also the only power source that can be moved by pistons, making them very useful.

any dust trail must either be air or a transparent block for the power to flow. Solid blocks here cut the power off. Slabs can be used, though, and the power will still flow.

Redstone power items like blocks and torches will power anything directly next to them, but not diagonally (without wire anyway).

For a more flexible setup, and an easy way to make

Adjacent blocks can be powered, but without help, diagonal blocks can't

Redstone lamps

Redstone lamps are bright lights that can be powered by a circuit. Very useful if you want to set up automated lighting in your home (especially when coupled with daylight sensors).

Dispensers

Dispensers are storage devices that will shoot out items when triggered. This includes supplies, and or offensive items like arrows.

Droppers

Droppers are devices that can drop or eject items when triggered. This can be useful if you want to push items into containers.

Hoppers

Hopped are used to funnel items to and from other containers or areas, such as chests.

Redstone repeaters

Redstone repeaters are used to repeat a power signal, boosting it and thus allowing power to travel longer distances beyond the 15 block limit. You can also use them to set 1-4 tick delays in the repeat process.

Redstone Comparators

These complex devices are used to compare the number of items in a container, and will either increase or reduce the power sent through them depending on this number.

Pistons

Pistons come in two varieties, normal and sticky. By default, when powered they extend, and when not powered they retract. This can allow the pushing of movable blocks (not all blocks are) and other tasks. Sticky pistons keep hold of the block they push and when they retract they pull the

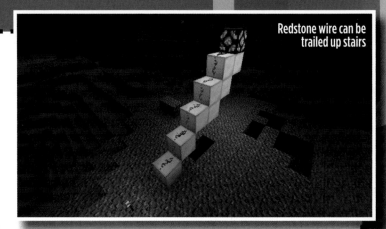

Redstone wire can be trailed up stairs

block back too, making them even more useful.

Switches

Switches come in various shapes and sizes, including actual switches, levers and pressure pads. They're all useful for activating devices.

Upstairs, Downstairs

It's easy to send power along a horizontal line, but building a circuit to provide power upwards and downwards isn't as easy, at least unless you know how. Redstone torches are the most flexible here, but wire can also manage.

For wire, you simply place the wire so if goes up a staircase of blocks. This can be straight or winding, whichever works. It's easy to do, but time and space consuming. Redstone torches are better.

Torches can carry power upwards through blocks (as well as upside-down slabs and stairs), and it makes it very easy to send power

There are many variations of Redstone torch towers, such as this one

vertically. Simply place a torch, then a block on top of it and then a torch on the new block. The second torch will be powered off, as adjacent torches reverse the state of the torch next to them. Repeat the process, and when high enough, do whatever you need with the power, such as a Redstone lamp, as seen here.

To send power downwards from a switch, you can use torches to power Redstone dust piles below them. Again, this alternates on and off as it descends, but it's an easy way to distribute power downwards, as seen here.

Basic Redstone circuit examples

Redstone circuits can be used for a huge number of tasks, and the sheer power at your fingertips is immense. Mastering them would take several volumes of guides, not to mention an education in electronics, but here are three examples of Redstone circuits to get you started.

Redstone torches and dust can send power current downwards

Simple circuit

We'll start with the most basic Redstone creation possible, a simple circuit that provides power to a light. All you need to do to create this is to place some Redstone wire on the ground leading up to a lamp, such as the Redstone lamp shown here, and place a Redstone torch at the

A very simple Redstone circuit turning on a Redstone lamp

other end. Viola! Instant powered light. Simple.

To add some functionality to your light, simply replace the Redstone torch with a lever. Levers and buttons can power Redstone devices. You can place a lever directly on some objects, such as the Redstone lamp, but if you want to set up ceiling mounted lights with a light switch next to the door, for example, this is how you'd do it.

Automatic lights

With Redstone Circuits you can create all sorts of automated devices, including lights that turn on during the night and off during the day. This is achieved by using a daylight sensor in conjunction with Redstone lamps and some circuitry. Simply place a daylight sensor outside and then add some Redstone wire leading to a sold block with a Redstone torch on the other side. Place the Redstone lamp above the torch and you're done. When it's daytime, the daylight sensor powers the wire, which turns off the Redstone torch. At night time, the sensor is deactivated, reactivating the torch, thus powering the Redstone lamp.

This simple light switch turns lights off during the day...

...g the night, all you need is wire connected to a daylight sensor outside

A simple Redstone clock which cycles the power around in circles endlessly

Redstone clocks

One of the most important, and much more complicated creations with Redstone circuits is the Redstone clock (or clock generator). Now, although these actually can be used to tell the time, the term clock isn't so much about time of day but instead about ticks, the measurement Redstone repeaters use to delay a power repeat. Once set up, these devices can loop a power signal in circles, with a delay set by you. This means you can set pistons to move in and out constantly, dispensers to fire at intermittent times and much, much more.

Creating a basic Redstone clock is easy enough, and uses Redstone wire, repeaters, a Redstone block, and a Redstone torch. To set up the clock, place some repeaters in a loop, ensuring the arrows point in the right direction, and leave the corners. Now, in the corners, place Redstone wire to connect the Repeaters

together in a circle of sorts. Off one of the corners place a Redstone block and then place the Redstone torch on the Redstone block. This powers the torch just long enough to get the clock going, but turns it off so it doesn't provide too much power to permanently power the whole circuit. If you've done this correctly, the circuit should now be cycling around in circles

By adjusting the repeater's settings, you can delay this signal by 1-4 ticks. Each tick in *Minecraft*'s code is around 1/20th of a second, and a Redstone tick is set at twice that, so at 2/20th of a second.

These clocks can be more and more complex, and using pistons, powered blocks and other circuitry tricks, you can create all sorts of elaborate devices. Let your imagination run wild.

Choo choo!

Another, even more simplistic way of creating

Mine cart clocks aren't as accurate, but are easier to understand and configure

a clock without repeaters is to use mine carts. This isn't quite as accurate, but it a little more customisable for those that can't get their heads around circuits. To create one, build a circular track, with enough powered rails to keep a mine cart going around in circles. Then, at one end place a rail track button, connected vis Redstone wire to something like a lamp or note block, and power the rail with a Redstone torch. Place the mine cart and get it moving. It'll now loop around and around, hitting the switch as it goes.

TNT

Another very important use for Redstone is with TNT. Redstone wire can be used to lay down a fuse for TNT, so you can detonate it from a safe distance. It can be set off by the usual methods of powering a wire, such as a lever, and with careful TNT use, you can quickly and easily blast away massive areas of land in seconds. It's also very satisfying. More TNT

packed together creates even larger explosions.

In fact, you can even use pressure pads and Redstone wire to set up explosive booby traps for enemy mobs, creating a deadly minefield around your home base or other tactically important area.

Slippery when wet

Redstone is a very flexible tool, but it's not much use under water. If water comes into contact with Redstone wire, it'll be washed away from the block it was laid on, breaking whatever circuit you laid. Instead, make use of Redstone Blocks. These can be used to power items underwater.

Redstone blocks can be used to power devices underwater, whilst torches and wire cannot

Redstone wire makes demolition a far safer task – BOOM!

ADVANCED MINING

Overground, Underground...

Generally speaking, the overground is a very safe place to wander, provided you stay indoors at night. By comparison, the underground is teeming with danger, whether from mobs, lava, long drops and falling gravel.

But you probably know that. The question is what can you do about it?

Creating an Underground Base is essential whenever you embark on any extended journey down a cave. A secure room where you can unload your stuff and recharge your batteries away from the constant attacks by skeletons and zombies is invaluable – not least because it dramatically lowers the chance that you'll die and lose everything you were carrying.

When mining for resources deep underground, the temptation to press on and find out what's behind that next block is absolutely huge – but if you don't turn around regularly and dump your hard-earned valuables in a safe place, you're eventually going to lose them all. Rather than going back to the surface every time can get tedious, but a small underground shelter stocked with chests should be just enough.

To build an underground shelter, you don't need to bring a large amount of resources. Wood is hard to reliably obtain underground, so bring a huge amount of that. Similarly, you should bring plenty of food to keep yourself going, although if you're really feeling ambitious you should bring eggs and seeds so that you can create a small farm.

As above ground, the absolute minimum a shelter requires is a bed and lighting to create a local spawn point and keep you safe while you're in it. Doors will keep out mobs, but also attract zombies, so you may want to create additional defences or use blocks instead of a normal door.

However, if you want your base to be useful, it also needs to be full of chests for storing items. Several furnaces wouldn't go amiss for cooking and smelting and, as mentioned earlier, you can use a combination of dirt, water and light-emitting blocks to create a small farm for growing extra food. The extremely stubborn may want to create a cavern big enough to plant a tree in to get renewable wood, but at this point it's probably quicker just to return to the surface.

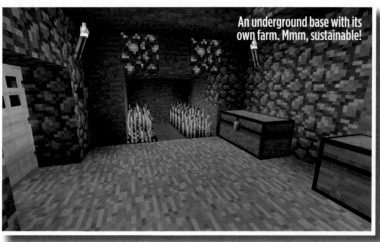
An underground base with its own farm. Mmm, sustainable!

Surfacing

At some point you have to get all the stuff you've mined back to the surface. We've got three ways you can do this...

The simplest and most direct way is to use Minecarts. By laying rails from the surface to your underground base, you'll be able to transport large amount of material virtually automatically. You can line up multiple minecart chests, and combine them with powered rails and carts so that they return to the surface without intervention. When you return yourself, they'll be waiting there for you to unload.

The main difficulty in this course of action is that making and laying track is very time-consuming. You may want to lay track as you explore, but it's usually more efficient to build your base and then mine a staircase to the surface so that you a direct route that uses as little track as possible. Just make sure your base hasn't been built under the ocean!

Minecarts are ideal for automating the process of moving resources above ground, particularly if you're mining great volumes of material or if there are multiple people mining in any given location. If it's just you, however, you may want to use an alternative method.

One of these alternatives is to use an Ender Chest, which you can create by wrapping an Eye of Ender in Obsidian using a crafting table. You'll need at least two – one for above ground and one for your base below it.

Ender Chests are incredibly useful for moving materials around in general, not just from below ground to above it, because all nether chests lead to the same storage area. This makes them ideally-suited to situations where a standard chest or minecart might get destroyed. Simply leave an Ender Chest in your main base above ground and take the second below ground with you. All you have to do is place resources in the underground chest, then once you get back to the surface you can quickly retrieve them from the overground chest.

The main downside to using Ender Chests is that you can only have one storage space per game, so they can only be used to transport a limited amount of material at a time. The good news is that you don't have to physically carry or move the resources you're transporting, so there's no danger of your hard-won valuables getting lost, stolen or destroyed in transit. Even if one chest is destroyed, the goods inside will be safe and accessible from the other.

If you're happy to move your goods physically, you could use a portal to shorten the journey. Every block you move through the Nether corresponds to eight blocks in the overworld, so you can cut a journey time dramatically – although you will be required to take a shortcut through an area filled with monsters and open yourself up to the possibility of monsters following you back.

Still, if this sounds like an attractive prospect, experiment with building portals to and from the Nether. It can take a while to get the hang of placing them properly, but once you've figured out a route between them in the Nether you can try and protect the pathway (a stone tunnel, for example) so that you minimise the risk of injury. Minecarts can also travel through portals, so if you want you can use them to minimise the amount of rails you place. Advanced users only!

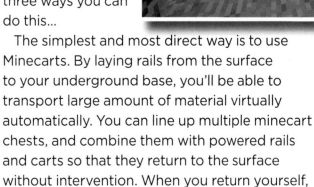

An example of a five-cart "train" – a powered cart at each end, two chests and a cart to ride in. First class all the way

A chicken in a minecart. Where it'll stay!

A Nether Chest. The simplest way to get items back to the surface

The basic components of an underground base. Surprisingly cosy, even with the iron doors

Minecart Tips

Although the basic minecart-and-rails mechanism is easy to create, there are many variations that you may can make use of to create increasingly complex systems. Empty minecarts can be combined with chests, furnaces, hoppers and TNT to create carts with differing properties, while rails can be made in powered or unpowered varieties. Experimenting with different types of rails will help you learn their properties, and redstone-powered rails are some of the simplest but most useful powered mechanisms in the game.

Empty carts can be ridden by players, making them one of the quickest forms of transport in the game. Mobs (both hostile and tame) and villagers can also get into empty minecarts if nudged correctly, and will remain there until the player dismounts them or the world is reloaded. Endermen cannot teleport out of minecarts, which makes them an effective way to trap them, but notably creepers can still explode while trapped in a minecart. Mobs and NPCs will not enter carts of their own volition, and even tamed mobs will walk alongside a player in a cart rather than get in with you.

To create a "train", place empty minecarts on a length of track with a short gap between them, then put a Powered Minecart (minecart + furnace) at either end. When you turn on one of the powered carts, the others will be pushed along, including the inactive powered cart. Using two powered carts enables you to push the train in any direction depending on which is active. Note that this only works on rails that are mostly flat, as powered carts have trouble pushing multiple carts up steep inclines.

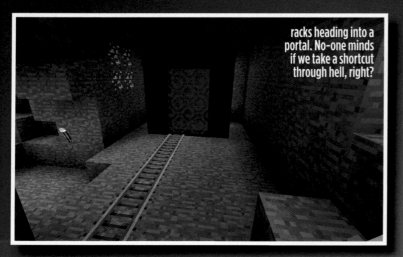

racks heading into a portal. No-one minds if we take a shortcut through hell, right?

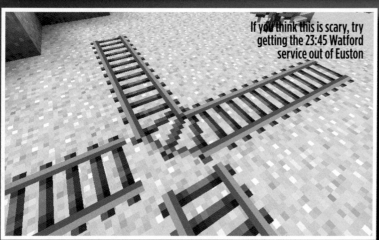

If you think this is scary, try getting the 23:45 Watford service out of Euston

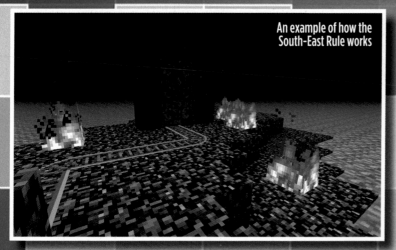

An example of how the South-East Rule works

This handy portal makes popping underground much less time-consuming

Railtrack Tips

Over flat ground, travelling in carts is about 20% faster than walking but 10% slower than sprinting. Travel in carts does have the benefit of being automated, however, which frees you up to fight, craft, or organise your inventory while in transit!

The larger a distance becomes, the more sense it makes to build tracks through portals and use the Nether as a shortcut. In the Overworld, carts travel at a speed of 8m/s over flat ground, but in the Nether they can travel an effective speed of 64 m/s, since one block in the Nether is worth 8 in the Overworld. This also uses vastly less track to cover the same distance. Just remember to take some arrows and armour!

Where rails cross, *Minecraft* will apply "the south-east rule", which states that the game favours this orientation over any other. Carts will therefore travel either south or east, depending on which of the two is perpendicular to their current direction. This does not apply if any rails lead downhill at an intersection, since downhill is always the preferred direction of a minecart.

Mobs will not cross rails unless they are chasing the player (or another mob/NPC) so rails can be used to "fence-off" areas from non-aggressive entities, such as animals and villagers, without obstructing the movement of players.

STRONGHOLDS

Like Abandoned Mines, Strongholds spawn naturally underground. Unlike Abandoned Mines, which are primarily important for their resources, it's necessary to find and successfully navigate a Stronghold in order to reach The End. That's because they're the only place in the game where you can find an End Portal. If you want to get there yourself, you'll have to follow our advice...

The all-seeing Eye of Ender. Er, I think it went that way

Locating and Navigating a Stronghold

Strongholds are difficult to find purely through exploration, partly due to their lack of external features but mainly because there's no requirement that they be connected to the surface. Luckily, strongholds are one of the few structures in the game that you can actively seek out. If you obtain an Eye of Ender and throw it into the air, it will naturally fly in the direction of the nearest End Portal. By following the trail, you can locate the area you need to dig into in order to find a Stronghold and the portal within.

Strongholds aren't a fixed size, but they are huge, occupying multiple levels and often branching out into cave systems and ravines. They are constructed of large rooms, stairwells and corridors, and it's very easy to become disorientated or lost. There are some common features, such as prison cells, fountain rooms and store rooms.

The most dangerous aspect of stronghold exploration is the abundance of silverfish, which can spawn and attack you when you mine one of the Stronghold's blocks, and if you reach the end portal where a Silverfish Spawner can be found. This is in addition to the normal mobs that spawn within the darkness! The hope is that you'll be encouraged to find the End Portal through exploration rather than carving through the stone, but bring good enough weapons and armour and you should be able to do it the easy way.

One of the rarer qualities of a Stronghold is that there are only three per world, regardless of its size. All three can be found anywhere between 640 and 1152 blocks from the original spawn point, and they will be distributed evenly to minimise the chance that a player can miss them. Remember this if you're trying to find one late in the game. You may have to head back towards the world's start point to reach one!

Finding strongholds without an Eye of Ender is basically impossible, and although you might get lucky it's a waste of time to actively look for one. Remember that Eye of Enders can be obtained by trading with Priests or by crafting together Blaze Power and an Ender Pearl.

Holding Down The Block

Finding a stronghold is useful in practical terms, but it also gives you access to a great number of resources. In particular, Stone Brick, Mossy Strong Brick and Cracked Stone Brick are difficult to come by elsewhere but plentiful in these fortresses. Metal railings and metal doors are also common in strongholds.

You can find chests in a stronghold with a variety of resources. As well as the usual mineral and metals, you can expect to find Paper, Books, Compasses, Apples, Armor, Maps and Ender Pearls. They also often contain a library, recognisable by its bookshelves, cobwebs and central "chandelier". Libraries can be one or two floors in height and contain one chest per floor, so when you see one, make sure to clean it out immediately!

Advanced Stronghold Exploration Tips

If you're planning a trip to The End, remember that Ender Portals require 12 Eyes of Ender to be activated but only contain between one and five by default. Eyes of Ender also have a one in five chance of shattering when thrown, so it's worth making sure you've got a plenty before beginning to explore a Stronghold.

Once well-lit, a Stronghold makes an excellent underground base thanks to their

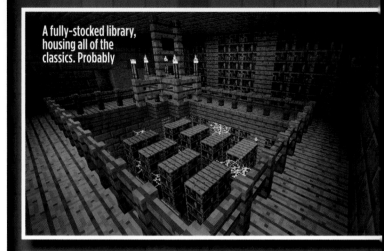

A fully-stocked library, housing all of the classics. Probably

layout and structure. Libraries can be easily converted into enchantment rooms, and cells into storage. The main disadvantage of this is that approximately 5% of all generated blocks in a Stronghold are actually Monster Egg blocks, which release Silverfish when broken.

It is possible to distinguish Monster Eggs from normal blocks because they break at a constant speed, and therefore may be quicker or slower to break than actual stone depending on the tool you're using and any enchantments. If you're fast enough, you can recognise that the block is breaking too fast and leave it alone. That said, you may prefer to simply kill the Silverfish that awakens.

Due to the presence of Silverfish, we recommend that you take a diamond sword with you into a Stronghold, since these can kill Silverfish in a single hit which will minimise the chance of a swarm. If you haven't got a diamond sword, a sufficiently powerful enchantment may achieve a similar effect.

An Ender Portal. The Stronghold's biggest secret

Just one of the many recurring rooms you'll see a lot of in a Stronghold

ABANDONED MINES

For a game about mining, *Minecraft* can sometimes seem suspiciously absent of actual mines. But deep beneath the overworld, there are abandoned mines to be found. Dug in the past by some long-forgotten miner, these labyrinthine structures are filled with resources, but frequently crawling with enemies. Exploring them can be great fun and rewarding in multiple ways – but make sure you read our guide first, or one of these mines could end up being your tomb!

Construction

Abandoned mines are normally hugely disordered and contain no logical layout or design. The sole exception is the mine "entrance", which is a dirt room that contains a flat floor, an arched ceiling and between one and four exits heading off in a different compass direction.

The exits lead to corridors carved through the stone which are 3x3 blocks in size. Resembling a real-world mine, corridors contain support structures to hold up the "roof" which consist of wooden fence posts and blocks of planks. Torches may light the way ahead.

If two corridors intersect, you may find a "crossing" feature, which are small square rooms often several floors high which contain large wooden pillars. Corridors may also contain small staircases, although they frequently lead nowhere interesting.

When generated, mine complexes can intersect with other geographical features, meaning it's not uncommon to discover a mine that crosses a ravine, or opens out into a large cave network. It's possible for two or even three mineshafts to generate partially on top of one another, leading to incredible fractured and hard to navigate mines, though ones rich with resources.

All Mine

Mines are a great place to top up on certain resources

The intersection of two corridors

A chest in a minecart in a mine

A staircase in a mine which, predictably, goes nowhere

without having to return to the surface. They're especially useful for harvesting wood underground, as it's very difficult to find any otherwise. For this reason, we recommend bringing a suitably strong axe. The amount of wood in a mine makes it likely the axe will break before you can harvest it all, so you may have to make several trips.

One of the most useful things about mines is that they contain naturally-occurring tracks, which you can pull up and re-use. This is far more efficient than crafting rails by hand, and a better use of your time! Tracks are found running down the centre of some corridors, and are frequently broken or disconnected, meaning they're not much use where they are.

You will also find chests and storage carts in abandoned mines which contain various types of loot. Food is common, and you're very likely to find bread, wheat and pumpkin or melon seeds. Resources like Iron, Coal, Redstone, Lapsis Lazuli and Gold are also frequently found in these chests, and if you're lucky, you may find diamonds, enchanted books or iron horse armour, although these items have a less than 3 in 80 chance of appearing.

The other main resource you can find in a mine is string, which is dropped when cobwebs are cut. Most mines contain several spider-spawners, so you can expect to pick up a lot of spider eyes as well. Finding and destroying the spawners early on is recommended, as it'll make collecting the other

resources much less stressful. Remember that swords and shears cut through cobwebs quicker than any other tool, and that fire can be used to quickly clear out the cobwebs around a spider-spawner.

Advanced Mine Exploration Tips

If you're trying to find a mine, it's a good idea to use ravines as a helpful look at what's going on under the surface. Mines are generated before ravines, so if the two intersect you'll be able to find corridors very easily by looking for wooden supports that have become exposed. It'll also help you find an easy way in!

Note that mineshafts are slightly less common near the original spawn point of your world. If you're specifically looking for one, try to travel a reasonable distance away first.

As with any large exploration task, it's a good idea to set up a local base before you venture too far in. The availability of wood and string makes it easy to create a small safe area with a bed – remember that string can be crafted into wool!

When building a base, make sure to block off the exits and keep the area well-lit, otherwise you'll almost certainly get attacked in the night. Spiders can fit through even single-block gaps, so don't leave any openings!

Most mines are incredibly hard to navigate due to the similarity of every passage and their illogical structure. If you do have a base to return to, you may want to use redstone to create a trail on the ground as you explore, or use signs to point the way back! Getting lost in a mine will leave you in a precarious situation. Who knows what's around the next corner!?

A minecart in a stairway that goes somewhere

SURVIVING DESERT TEMPLES

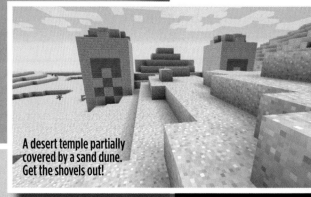

A desert temple partially covered by a sand dune. Get the shovels out!

Temples that spawn in the desert appear as large pyramids constructed out of sandstone blocks with two towers either side of the entrance, although they are occasionally obscured by sand dunes on several sides. As in real life, these temples hide riches and dangers in equal measure and are a prime target for the adventurous looter. As long as you can survive long enough to get in and out, that is...

Just Deserts

Getting into desert temples is simple enough with even the most basic pickaxe. All you have to do is make sure you aren't crushed by falling sand at any point and you'll soon reach the interior chamber, which contains a block of blue wool at the centre. In the absence of any X, this wool marks the spot where treasure can be found. Specifically, that means four chests, brimming with rare items.

But don't touch anything yet! Beneath the block of wool there lies a large pit, and at the base of the pit are the chests and a pressure pad which, when activated, will detonate nine hidden blocks of TNT: enough to blow you, the treasure and much of the temple sky high.

To retrieve the goodies below, you can either walk to the edge of the main chamber and dig downwards through the sandstone, aiming for the hidden pit, or use a water bucket to create a spring that'll allow you to swim to the bottom of the pit. Either way, take care not to activate the pressure pad once you're down there!

There's Treasure Everywhere: Temple Tips

Temples are the only place in *Minecraft* where TNT blocks spawn, and while they're hard to collect you can potentially get your hands on them by using a pickaxe with the light touch enchantment. Try to keep one with you when exploring a temple!

Rare items found in Desert Temple chests include Enchanted Books, Horse Armor, Emeralds and Diamonds, although you're also likely to find Iron, Gold, Rotten Flesh, Saddles and Bones.

One problem with desert temples is that because the lower pit is dark, mobs can spawn inside and set off the TNT before you reach it. We recommend that you disarm a temple as soon as you discover it, even if you don't take the items with you first time.

SURVIVING
JUNGLE TEMPLES

Temples that spawn in the Jungle are often hard to find due to the density of the biome's foliage, but the daring explorer can treat themselves to considerable riches found with the cobble- and moss stone structures. Although Jungle Temples aren't as explosive as Desert Temples, they do contain more traps, as well as a puzzle to solve, and are best approached with care.

The Mighty Jungle

Jungle temples contain three floors. On the lower floor, you'll find a randomised puzzle room with three levers connected to three pistons which you must solve to open a secret door to reveal a treasure chest.

There are two possible sequences that solve the puzzle which depend on the location of the levers as you walk down the temple stairs. Levers on the left are solved by pressing Right, Left, Left, Right and Levers on the right are solved by pressing Left, Right, Right, Left.

Once you've solved the puzzle, continue through the temple, watching out for tripwires which activate arrow-filled dispensers. The tripwires are often obscured by vines, so take things slow to avoid activating them by accident. You can permanently disarm the tripwires by breaking them using shears only (anything else will set them off).

When you reach the end of the hall you should find a second chest with a tripwire directly in front of it. Break it and loot the chest, then leave at your leisure.

Low-Hanging Fruit: Temple Tips

Jungle temples are excellent places to mine components for mechanisms, since they contain levers, string, pistons and other useful parts. They also contain Moss Stone, which is a fun block aesthetically.

Note that the chests themselves contain the same items as those found in the desert temples, although in this case each temple only contains two chests and so fewer items overall.

The dispensers that form the arrow traps can also be raided, allow you to obtain up to 18 free arrows. If you empty the dispenser before the tripwire is broken, it won't be able to shoot arrows at you when it is!

Since temples are often obscured by leaves, you may want to automate your search for a temple by lighting a sufficiently large fire. Not the most ecologically-minded way to go about your business, but effective nonetheless.

Once you know the location of the chests within a Jungle Temple, you might choose to mine your way to them from the outside. This is a useful technique if a tree has spawned inside a temple and replaced blocks in the mechanism, rendering it unsolvable.

The interior of a jungle temple. Who built it, and why? We may never know

ESSENTIAL MULTIPLAYER TIPS

For many *Minecraft* is a solo experience, where the involvement of others involves showing them the stuff built with their own digital hands. But playing *Minecraft* online, either with like-minded friends or with strangers who just happen to love *Minecraft,* is hugely popular and often produces some of the most awe-inspiring constructions possible. That's the benefit of teamwork! It also makes the process of exploring that great big world less lonely.

Of course, Multiplayer also comes with its own unique considerations. Not everything in the world is yours for the taking: it's not just your sandbox any more! Accidentally triggering a creeper and blowing a hole in a building changes from "annoying, I shall have to fix that" to "...I hope no one saw me". And there's always the possibility that items left in an unmarked chest may be taken by another player.

For that reason we've assembled this list of essential tips and tricks to help you start or join an online Minecraft server and focus your energies on what's most fun.

Joining a Server

The most fundamental aspects of multiplayer

Minecraft etiquette have to be around respect and communication.

The former means respecting what other players have built and the items they've stored within. Don't modify a building's layout because you think it could be done better another way. If you really want to make such a point, build your own home with the jacuzzi in the east wing instead of the west!

Respecting what other players have built means they will respect what you've built. It's much like real life, especially since some *Minecraft* servers demand the digital equivalent of planning permission.

Any items that have been stashed within a building should be considered the property of whoever built it. Sure those diamonds look tempting, and you might think that if whoever mined them really wanted them they'd keep them to hand... but for all you know they might be off exploring the Nether and hoping to avoid dropping rare items on death!

Sometimes generous players will provide chests full of items that they're happy for people to take. In such

Your first visit to a multiplayer server may involve a foyer like this

11

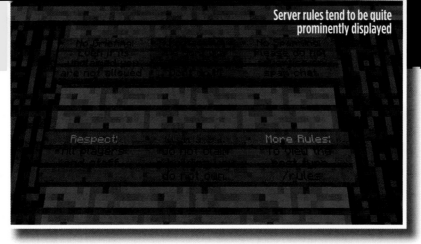

Server rules tend to be quite prominently displayed

instances you're certain to find a sign placed nearby that says as much. If there's no sign, it's a fair assumption that those goodies aren't up for grabs.

Speaking of signs, some players don't like people trespassing on their private property and may mark areas as off limits. There's technically nothing to stop you from ignoring such instructions but some servers take this sort of thing very seriously, and there's the possibility that you could get banned for disobeying. It may seem harsh, but whoever runs the server can set whatever rules they like.

As for those server rules, chances are they'll be displayed both when you log in, and also wherever you found the details for the server itself! Reading the server rules is important: they'll generally list a very specific set of considerations for all players to abide by. These vary from server to server but they'll generally include items like no stealing, no griefing, and read the signs.

If you've only played solo *Minecraft* you may be unfamiliar with the chat function. On PC, it's accessed by pressing the forward slash key (/). Chat messages will appear in the bottom left of your screen, and they may sometimes contain information worth reading. Often it'll just be people chattering. If you're new to the server it's best just to let them get on with it while you work out who everyone is, but if you do want to request they stop 'flooding' the chat, be polite.

Many PC *Minecraft* servers are set up to allow voice chat using a microphone, and this is the only means of chatting on the Xbox Live version. The main rule to bear in mind here is that often everyone can hear you by default, but they may not want to! Try and restrict voice chat to sensible communications, and also make sure that there's no background noise that will be picked up that might irritate players. The latter could include someone hoovering, people talking loudly nearby or even a passing samba band. Delete as applicable.

When it comes to finding a server, make sure you choose one that is right for you. Some servers offer a standard *Minecraft* survival experience whereas others involve role-playing or allow player-versus-player combat. There are servers out there that involve players participating in the Hunger Games or simulating life in an Imperial Roman city. There's something out there for everyone.

How to find a server, you ask? No version of *Minecraft* has an in-game server browser right now, and while that may change in future Mojang's own Realms service is still under development, so we won't be seeing such a feature any time soon. For now, online *Minecraft* communities are the way to go. There are a lot

Some foyers are m
extravagant than oth

of popular *Minecraft* forums online which can be a good place to start, or there are entire websites dedicated to helping players find servers such as minecraft-server-list.com.

Hosting a Server

Hosting your own server can be a great way of focusing your creative energies on a world that you can exercise some authorial control over whilst still allowing others to participate. It's also a more expensive option than simply joining an existing server, so it's not the right way to go for everyone.

You can of course build your own server for playing *Minecraft*, but with the game and its worlds being fairly resource-heavy – and the know-how required to build a server being considerable – it's often easier just to rent one. This also has the advantage of being something you can cancel if you and your friends get bored!

There are a lot of companies out there today offering dedicated servers for gaming, with *Minecraft* being one of the top games such companies support, so shop around and find the best deal you can from a company that

seems reputable. Multiplay are a popular option, and in the future Mojang's own Realms service will probably be reliable and trustworthy too.

A third option is to host a game on your home network. This is good if you just want to play with family members or housemates and aren't bothered about anyone outside your home getting involved. It does involve a bit of fiddling about to get it working, but you can find what you need on the official site: minecraft.net/download

Assuming you're not playing on a LAN, consider setting up either 'whitelists' or 'blacklists' so you can control who has access to your server. A whitelist lets you specify players who are allowed access – this is the safest option as you can allow only your friends' accounts. A blacklist specifies players who are not allowed access – if you have trouble with a particular griefer you can block them in this way, but that won't stop anyone else coming in and causing trouble!

When it comes to unwanted guests crashing your party, you can always try and dodge this bullet entirely by considering where you advertise your shiny new *Minecraft* server. If you post the details on a public forum, anyone can see it. If you post it to a private group or chat session, then you know that only those you told and anyone they told in turn will know about your server. This does help reduce the risk of griefer invasions!

Last but not least: play safe, and have fun!

The first moments on a server can be confusing, but stick with it

BUILDING BEACONS

Beacons are player-created structures that have two primary uses: as a local navigation aid, and to give power-ups to nearby players. They can only be created after a considerable amount of valuable resources are collected and using certain rare items, and for that reason they won't typically be within reach of a player for some time after starting a game. It isn't necessary to build a Beacon to reach The End and "complete" the game, but they do make a fun late-game goal in their own right!

Beacon Bits

Beacons are created by crafting valuable minerals into blocks, arranging them into a solid pyramid up to four levels high, then placing a beacon block on top. You can use four materials to create the pyramid: Diamond, Emerald, Gold or Iron, in any combination. Once the beacon is active it will emit a beam of blue light up into the sky which is visible from

The crafting recipe for a beacon. Remember to ask an adult to collect a Nether Star for you

up to 170 blocks away. When a beacon is active, you'll be able to choose the effects it emits. Larger pyramids have a greater range (from 20 up to 50 blocks) and the effects will be applied every few seconds.

The most important part of a Beacon is the Beacon Block. To create one of these you'll need to craft Obsidian, a Nether Star and Glass as shown in the screenshot. In Survival mode, Nether Stars can only be obtained by killing the Wither, and are therefore one of the rarest items in the game. If you get a Nether Star, do your best to hang onto it, as they can be difficult to replace!

Building a beacon's pyramid takes a long time itself. The minimum size (one level) pyramid requires nine blocks of mineral in a 3x3 configuration, so you'll need to collect 81 ingots/gems to build. By comparison, a four level pyramid requires 1,476 ingots/gems to create the 164 blocks needed (a 9x9 base, up to a 3x3 peak).

Powers

When a beacon is active, players can activate its powers by placing a resource in its empty slot (similar to how you would operate a furnace or anvil). You will then be able to select the effect to apply from a list. Beacons four levels high can also apply a secondary effect. The item you use to select a beacon's power will be consumed, and you must use another item in order to alter the effect.

The available power effects are speed (move faster), Haste (mine faster), Resistance (improved armor), Jump Boost (more powerful jump) and Strength (increased melee damage). When selecting a secondary effect, you can also choose Regeneration, which restores health. Note that single and double-level pyramids cannot access the full range of powers, only those three levels and above can provide all five.

Beacon Locations

The smart player knows to place Beacons in places where they will have the best effect. Here are some of our suggestions.

Haste, Speed and Jump Boost are most efficiently applied in areas where you're likely to mine blocks and move around a lot. If you can get these beacons to activate underground, you can vastly improve the speed at which you collect resources, but remember to build them no deeper than 50 levels from bedrock so as to take full advantage of the effect influence.

Strength, Regeneration and Resistance are most useful in areas where you're likely to be attacked, so it's advisable to keep them close to your base. Create several beacons and apply all three of these effects to an area to help create a "mob farm" so that you can trap and kill monsters with as little risk to yourself as possible.

Advanced Tips

When building multiple beacons, be aware that the pyramids can overlap. By extending the top level to accommodate additional Beacon Blocks at least two blocks apart, you can gain all six possible beacon effects at the maximum range using just 244 resource blocks – although collecting multiple nether stars could pose a problem!

Beacons can't be activated underground or indoors unless the sky above them is visible and has a light level of at least 15. This can be achieved underground by opening skylights. Some transparent blocks, such as glass, won't obstruct a beacon's activation, although water does.

Note that Lava, which the game considers a "transparent" block, doesn't prevent the activation of a beacon. You can therefore use strategically-placed lava to protect a beacon from attack by other players or mobs.

When constructing the pyramid for a beacon, it makes sense to prioritise the use of Iron over any other resource. The materials the pyramid is constructed from have no effect on the beacon other than determining how it looks, so rarer items such a diamond and emerald are better employed elsewhere in the game.

Beacons emit light. Good news at sundown!

BEATING THE ENDER DRAGON

Getting to the End

Although you'll spend the majority of your time in *Minecraft* exploring the overworld and building all sorts of creations, not to mention mining the depths for diamonds, in Survival mode there's a main reason for your efforts – finding and defeating the Ender Dragon. This is the main 'boss' of *Minecraft* and it's a very tough challenge.

To actually get to The End, the world where the Ender Dragon and an army of Endermen lurk, you'll need to locate and activate an Ender portal, this is what a lot of your foraging and building has all been about. To do this you have to perform some very specific tasks (or you could just switch to Create mode and build a portal, but that's cheating).

First, you need to progress far enough in the game to get to the Nether (so you'll need diamond and obsidian). Once in the Nether, you'll need to kill several Blazes to acquire Blaze Rods. You'll need at least six Blaze Rods, but gathering more is advisable for spares, and if you want to brew potions.

You'll then need to return to the overworld and find some Endermen to slay. Each one killed should yield an Ender Pearl. You'll need at least 12 of these. Once you have them, you need to craft 12 Eyes of Ender. This is done by turning your Blaze Rods into Blaze Powder (you'll get two powders per rod) and then using an Ender Pearl and Blaze Powder to craft an Eye of Ender.

When you have these, head to the surface and throw an Eye of Ender. It'll head in the direction of the nearest stronghold. Keep doing this until you zero in on a stronghold and dig down to it. Once in the stronghold (more tips on these can be found in the stronghold section of this guide), locate the End Portal room and place your Eyes of Ender into the slots on the portal. Once all are placed, the portal will open and you can jump into The End. But before you do, you'll need to make sure you have the right equipment.

What to bring

There are a few essential supplies you need to take with you if you want to slay the Ender Dragon. First grab some armour, enchanted armour at that. At least iron armour, and enchant it with Protection IV. If you've got some diamond armour, all the better.

For attacking your best friend here will be a bow, again enchanted. Ideally you should utilise Power III as this gives you the best attack strength against the boss (it'll drop with around 12 charged shots to the head). Infinity is also useful, as it gives you around 385 shots before it breaks.

Although not as useful against the Ender Dragon, a sword is always handy, ideally enchanted with Fire. Although sword enchantments hardly affect the dragon (and it's immune to fire anyway), the fire power will pacify any enraged Endermen.

Next up are potions, and you'll need a stack of these, particularly Splash Potions of Healing II and Potions of Regeneration. Splash Potions

Ender Dragon

The End is a desolate place filled with Endermen and the mighty Ender Dragon

Your game mode has been updated

of Healing II can regenerate four hearts instantly, and the regeneration potions will slowly regenerate up to 24 hearts over two minutes. This should ensure you're kept at full health.

You'll need to bring plenty of blocks to build a bridge over to the main island, as you'll often appear on an obsidian platform away from the mainland.

Other equipment you need isn't as essential, but highly advisable. Any spare Ender Pearls are useful as they let you teleport around, and are very

useful for actually reaching the main island in The End if you don't want to use blocks. A diamond pickaxe can be used to dig out of the ground if you spawn in it, which can happen a lot, and always have some food on you to keep your stamina up – you'll be doing a lot of running.

It's also very wise to bring some obsidian with you. This is the only block from the overworld that the Ender Dragon can't destroy, and it's very useful for building shelters in the console versions. It can make your life a lot easier.

The End

Okay, so you've arrived at The End. As you'll see, it's a very barren, and dark place. There are few block types here and no day or night cycle. End Stone forms much of the world, obsidian pillars dot the landscape, with Ender Crystals mounted on top.

Endermen can bee seen everywhere and that big black thing in the sky is the Ender Dragon itself. You'll notice a handy health bar for the dragon at the top of the screen. Welcome to your biggest challenge yet.

Before you can get started, though, you may need to

It won't take long for the Ender Dragon to spot you and begin its onslaught

Ender Crystals heal the Ender Dragon

Arrows are the easiest way to destroy Ender Crystals

actually reach the mainland. To do this you can build a bridge, tricky when being attacked by the Ender Dragon, or you can use Ender Pearls to teleport.

Be very careful in The End, as there's a deadly drop into an endless void all around, and if you die here, you'll lose all of your items and respawn back in the overworld. The only ways to leave The End are to die, or to beat the Ender Dragon and leave via the End Portal.

The Ender Dragon's tactics
The Ender Dragon is a hugely powerful mob, and is dangerous due to its powerful attacks and its ability to fly around, making it hard to damage. It's also aided by those glowing crystals on the obsidian pillars. As it flies past, these crystals heal the dragon, negating any damage you do.

The dragon behaves a little differently between PC and console, with the console version being able to spit Ender Acid, which behave in a similar way to Ghast fireballs. The PC version has no projectile.

The Dragon will attempt to hit you, and dives down towards

you to do damage. It can destroy any block it comes into contact with, except for End Stone, obsidian and bedrock.

How to beat it
Although you don't actually have to, it's usually best to first focus your attention on the Ender Crystals on the obsidian pillars. Without these, the Ender Dragon can't regenerate health, making your fight much easier, not to mention shorter.

You can destroy these with a single sword hit or arrow shot. As the crystals are on top of obsidian pillars, this means a well aimed arrow is preferable, otherwise you can build your way up and hit them. Jump-building is the best way to do this. It should be noted that destroying an Ender Crystal while the Ender Dragon is being healed by it will actually damage the dragon.

Console player will also have to contend with some of the crystals being surrounded by iron bars, making an arrow strike impossible. These need to be built up to and destroyed at close quarters. Once all the Ender Crystals are destroyed,

you can turn your attention to the dragon.

Once again, your bow is the key here, and you'll need to be both accurate, and quick-footed. The Ender Dragon is very difficult to hit at a distance, and so the best way to damage it is from close range. So, wait until the dragon swoops down to attack and let him have it with an arrow to the face. If you hit it with a charged arrow, it should pull up. If not, you'll need to quickly dodge out of the way if you can. If you take damage, be sure to heal if needed and then repeat the process. The dragons needs to circle before each attack, so you should have time to heal.

Eventually, the Ender Dragon will explode, and the End portal will appear below it (on console, it'll already be in the middle of the world, but won't activate until the dragon is dead). You'll get a whole heap of experience too, so don't forget to pick it all up.

The Dragon Egg and End portal
When the Ender Dragon is a goner, the End Portal will be active, and atop it you'll see the fabled Dragon Egg block. This is

Arrows are the safest way to attack the dragon

A purple explosion heralds the Ender Dragon's demise

a totally useless block for now, with no actual use other than a trophy. It's also tricky to acquire as it teleports once hit, and it's easy to lose. There's only one Dragon Egg per world, making it the rarest bock in the game.

To grab it, you can use various methods, but the following two are the easiest. First, cover up the End Portal to stop the egg falling in and then place a piston next to the egg and activate it. The piston will push the egg, causing it to drop as a collectable resource. Simply walk over it to pick it up.

The second method exploits the egg's obedience of gravity. If the egg falls onto a non solid block, such as a torch, it'll turn into a collectable resource. So, you can destroy the block two blocks below it and place a torch, then destroy the block between

The End Portal will appear/activate after the Ender Dragon is dead, and sports a Dragon Egg

and the egg will fall onto the torch. Easy. This isn't possible here, as the portal is made of bedrock, but once you have the egg and return to the overworld, this is a useful tactic.

Once you have the egg, it will behave like most other blocks, and you can use it for decoration, and to boast to your friends that you've beaten the Ender Dragon. Once placed, however, it'll go back to teleporting when hit, so the same methods apply if you want to pick it up again.

A simple piston mechanism is all it takes to easily collect the Dragon Egg

With egg in hand, all you need to do is jump into the End Portal and you'll be treated to the End Poem, the reward for reaching the 'end' of *Minecraft*. Enjoy, and well done!

Essential tips

One of the biggest problems you face when fighting the Ender Dragon are the Endermen. Accidentally looking at them, which is easy to do whilst fighting the dragon, will provoke them. This means you'll

have multiple foes attacking you. To avoid this, you can travel to the End wearing a pumpkin on your head. This doesn't provide any protection, and also obscures your view somewhat, but you can stare at Endermen as much as you like and they won't attack.

Arrows blessed with a fire enchantment can make aiming at the Ender Crystals much easier.

On console, the Ender Dragon cannot go through obsidian or bedrock. If you build a shelter out of obsidian, anything inside should be safe. This doesn't apply to PC.

Always fight the Ender Dragon on solid ground away from the edge of the world. Its attacks causes knockback, and you can be sent flying to your doom. This includes trying to fight the dragon from atop an obsidian pillar as falling from such a height is fatal.

To climb the pillars use soft blocks like dirt (but not gravity-affected blocks like sand), as it's easier to destroy and descend back to ground level when you've taken care of an Ender Crystal.

If you're having trouble, simply get some friends to come and help you. The Ender Dragon is far easier when attacked *en masse*, and if you die, your friends can grab your items so you don't lose them (unless you're knocked into the void).

Jump into the End Portal to finish your quest

SUMMONING AND BEATING THE WITHER

Summoning the Wither

Unlike the Ender Dragon, *Minecraft*'s second boss mob isn't simply waiting around for you to wander through a portal and attack it. If you're going to face the Wither, you're going to have to summon it first. Your repayment? A whole lot of pain, unless you know how to take it on.

Before you can try to battle the Wither, you'll need the items to summon it, and these are gathered from the Nether. You're going to need (per Wither summon) four blocks of Soul Sand and three Wither skulls. Now, the first of these, the Soul Sand, is easy to get as it can be found all over the Nether. The Wither skulls, however, aren't quite so easy, as you have to kill Wither skeletons, each of which can drop Wither skulls. This isn't always guaranteed, as it's a rare drop.

So you'll need to hunt and kill a number of Wither skeletons, which you can find in Nether fortresses. To give yourself a better chance of finding Wither skulls, use a sword with the Looting enchantment as this increases the possibility of rare drops. When you have the Soul Sand and Wither skulls, you're ready for the Wither.

Preparation

Just as you should before you fight the Ender Dragon, ahead of your fight against the Wither, make sure you have the right equipment, Arguably more so than with the Ender Dragon, for this fight you're going to need rock solid defence and some powerful attack, as the Wither is, certainly on hard difficulty, the most powerful mob in the game and has the most health. It's even more powerful than the Ender Dragon, boasting 300 health points.

So, it goes without saying that some enchanted diamond armour is a must, with Protection IV. This enchantment also protects against the Wither effect, which is a must. Even with this protection you'll need plenty of healing, so bring plenty of Instant Health II Splash Potions and also some Strength II potions to enhance your melee attacks by 260%. Food is also a must, if possible a few enchanted golden apples.

For weapons you'll need a diamond sword enchanted with Smite V, and a bow with Power V. Infinity is also helpful. It'll take a good deal of

This simple shape is how you summon the Wither

The Wither's spawn explosion is very powerful, so stay away

Fighting the Wither

Fighting the Wither is a long two-stage process, and it constantly regenerates health, so you need to keep on it at all times. For the first 50% of its health, it's best to let the Wither have it with arrows. Keep your distance, and try to avoid its powerful projectiles. Keep healing as and when needed and keep your regeneration effect going, you'll need the extra health boost.

After a while, when the Wither has around half its health left, it'll form a blue shield and become immune to arrows. At this point you need to unsheathe your diamond sword. You'll do plenty of damage with the Smite V enchantment, and as long as you keep tabs on your health, you'll put the Wither down quickly enough. Once it's dead, don't forget to pick up the Nether Star, which is used to make beacons. Sadly, you'll only get 50 experience per Wither, which isn't much at all.

arrows to take on the Wither, so bring three full stacks if you don't have the Infinity enchantment for the bow.

Summoning the Wither

Okay, so you're ready to do battle with the terror that is the Wither, and it's time to summon it. First, get to an area well away from any important places, such as your home base. The Wither will do untold damage to anything nearby if you don't kill it, so be careful. You can summon the Wither in the Nether too, which will keep the overworld safe, but the foes in the Nether can make it an even more difficult fight. You can even summon it in The End, but the Endermen can also make it tricky.

To actually summon the Wither, place the Soul Sand in a T shape, and then place each Wither skull on top. As soon as you place the last skull (skulls must be placed last or the summon will fail), the Wither will start to power up. At this point, run! Get some distance between you and the Wither as a huge explosion will be triggered when the Wither is at full strength, destroying everything in its range, including obsidian blocks.

The Wither will now be fully summoned, and it'll begin to fly around, spreading destruction wherever it goes by firing explosive Wither Skull projectiles. It'll attack any non-undead mob on sight, including, of course, you. Time to give it what for.

Easy Wither kill

Arguably, the easiest way to kill a Wither requires only a piston and a lever, and a trip to the Nether. First, head to the Nether and dig upward until you hit the bedrock ceiling. You'll need a 3x3 area of bedrock in the ceiling, with an air block in the space above the bedrock. Now, ensure there's a three block high space between the ground and the bedrock ceiling. Dig a hole and place an upward-facing piston in it and the lever next to it.

Build the Wither structure on top of the piston, so that the skulls are just below the bedrock ceiling. As soon as the Wither appears, hit the lever. This will push the Wither into the ceiling, meaning it can't move or attack. Get your sword ready and defend just in case some of the explosion hits you (which it shouldn't as the Bedrock stops it), then simply swing away, without fear of reprisal.

SURVIVING HARDCORE

Hardcore

Hardcore mode is a variant on *Minecraft*'s normal Survival mode, but has one major difference – you get one life. Yes, if you die in Hardcore mode that's it, game over. You can't respawn, and the world is even deleted. It's a one shot deal, and to make matters worse, the game is locked into hard difficulty, and you can't even use bonus chests. This is for the *Minecraft* elite only.

Obviously, this isn't a mode for the new *Minecraft* player, or casual gamer. This mode was implemented for those looking for the ultimate *Minecraft* challenge, not to mention those with endless patience. Can you imagine fighting all the way to the Ender Dragon and dying, only to have to start all over again? Yes, it could be just a tad frustrating. However, if you relish this kind of Rogue-style play, this is the mode for you.

Death in Survival

When you die in a normal game of *Minecraft*, you'll get the option to respawn or return to the title screen. This either drops you back into the world at your last spawn point, or saves the world and returns you to the title. In Hardcore this isn't the case.

When you die here all you get is a game over screen with a button to delete the world. Once you click this, the world is gone and you need to start over.

The ultimate Minecraft challenge is Hardcore

Die in Hardcore, and that's it, your world is deleted

If you play Hardcore on a multiplayer server, you'll get a game over message and then have to leave the server.

You'll also get a banned message, with the reason for the ban being dying on Hardcore. If you attempt to rejoin the server, you'll be barred.

Survival tips

You should adhere to many of the same tips as in normal survival mode when playing Hardcore, but due to the single life, there are things you need to be even more vigilant about. For one, until you're totally prepared, with the right supplies, never go out at night time. On

Die in an online Hardcore server, and you'll be disconnected and not let back on

That beautiful world hides permanent danger in Hardcore mode

hard mobs spawn everywhere at night, and death awaits around every corner.

Make sure your shelter is easy to find and well lit. This means you'll not get lost and can run home if you're in danger. The light will also prevent mob spawns. Always find material to make a bed so you can skip night entirely.

Become familiar with the various ways to build emergency hiding places, such as cliff side shelters, holes in the floor and so on. If you're away from home at night, always seek shelter instead of trying to brave the dangerous small hours.

Creepers take on a whole new level of terror on Hardcore, and they're the most common cause of instant death. For this reason, and many more, always keep a constant lookout around you. Whether you're mining, chopping down trees or simply exploring, always look around in every direction.

When it comes to farming, if you can, build an indoor farm. Enough light will let most things grow, such as crops and trees, and you can always build a greenhouse out of glass blocks. This way, you won't have to expose yourself to mobs and/or skeleton arrows by farming outside.

Although we advised against the use of armour for the most part in survival earlier in the guide, when in Hardcore you should always have some form of protection. Anything

that helps keep you alive is important. Iron armour is the best as it's easy enough to get. As soon as you can get diamond armour, though, go for it.

Buckets of water are always essential, regardless of difficulty, but even more so here, and putting yourself out if you're on fire is one of the primary uses. Also, always have a bucket or two of milk on hand so you can cure poison and other negative effects. Be careful, though, as milk will also remove beneficial effects.

Falling is deadly in most difficulties, and if you can respawn, it's not so bad. In Hardcore, though, it's game over, so a bucket of water can help if you're quick enough, as pouring it can make a waterfall that can stop you from falling to your doom.

You'll always need a good stock of food on hand to keep that hunger meter full. Without this you won't regenerate health and you won't be able to sprint, which is as deadly as a mob on Hardcore. As soon as you see some animals when starting a new world, kill them to get some food right away, and harvest crops for always useful and easy to amass bread.

When playing normal Survival, it's easy to get in the habit of storing away important items for use later, in case you die. Saving things like diamond armour and pickaxes is common, but on hardcore is pointless. If you die, it's game over, so there's no reason to save up your items. Use them as soon as you get them.

Caves are a great way for early players to find ore normally, but in Hardcore they're one of the worst places to go early on due to plentiful enemy mobs and potential easy deaths. Until you're sufficiently prepared, always stick to your own self-excavated mines. With these you have control over them and can avoid dangerous fights. If you dig out into a natural cave or disused mineshaft, retreat and come back when you're better prepared.

Some biomes make it far easier to survive than others. Flatlands, for example, are far easier to stay alive in than jungles due to the increased visibility, and less likely chance of ambush. Of course, this also means resources are limited, but they can make safer homesteads. Mushroom biomes are potentially the safest of all, as enemy mobs can't spawn on or below them. Sadly, mushroom biomes sport very few resources, apart from Mooshrooms, which can be used as an infinite supply of mushroom stew.

Allies like wolves and golems are always useful, even on easier difficulties, but on Hardcore they really can be a lifesaver. Exploring with a pack of wolves can be excellent protection, and taking cats with you can deter Creepers, eliminating the most common cause of death. Leash an Iron Golem and you've got a very powerful bodyguard.

Don't even think of travelling to the Nether until you've got plenty of supplies, food, good armour and decent weapons. The Nether is the land of unexpected doom, and when one life is all you have, being unprepared is simply foolish.

Pick your fights very carefully at all times. If you don't need to harvest mob drops, then don't even bother fighting if you don't have to. Some foes are always best avoided altogether, even if they have good drops. Zombie Pigmen, for example, should be avoided at all costs. If you anger one, you'll be mobbed by an army of pigmen, and you'll probably die in seconds. Don't tempt this fate.

To increase your chances of surviving Hardcore, it's often best to play online with friends. This won't bring you back if you die, but the more of you there are, the more eyes you have watching each other's backs. In battle, there's more than one target for mobs to go for, and a group of stronger than a single person.

If you survive long enough to get to The End you'll only get one shot, so do everything you possibly can to make sure you're prepared. It's worth taking a lot longer to get the right enchantments and plentiful supplies, so don't rush it.

Hotbar configuration

Every *Minecraft* player has their own favourite hotbar configuration, but on Hardcore it's useful to order items in a certain way.

From left to right it's a good idea to place items as follows: sword, bow, pickaxe, axe, shovel, food, solid blocks, torches, bucket. The reason for this configuration is that the sword and bow are always easy to get to (it's best to always have your sword selected when exploring), and a quick selection input can get to buckets of water if needed. Food is useful in the hotbar, but not essential as you can find a safe spot to eat.

Cheating Hardcore

Although the idea of Hardcore is to purposely enforce a real-life limit of a single death, there are ways around this so you can at least retain your world. The easiest method is to simply backup your save game, which includes your world. You can find this in X:\Users\ USERNAME\AppData\Roaming\.minecraft\ saves (where X is your install drive and USERNAME your Windows logon). Back this up to another location by copying it, and you can then restore it if needed. This can be very useful before doing particularly dangerous tasks like visiting the Nether or taking on the Ender Dragon.

Of course, doing this does defy the point of playing Hardcore in the first place, and it may be easier to simply play the game in Survival mode on hard. Then again, it's your game, and you play how you like.

MODDING

Vanilla *Minecraft* is chock (or should that be block?) full of content to explore, discover, harvest, collect and build with, and is a perfectly playable game on any platform. It was also a PC game first, and the PC has a well-deserved reputation for the size and creativity of its game modding communities. *Minecraft* – the biggest indie game in the world – is no exception!

Mods available for the game range from minor tweaks in performance or visuals, all the way through to major additions to gameplay or world generation, not to mention unique maps or total conversions based around unique gameplay.

The following pages will explain how to mod the game and then what some of our favourite mods are, including both minor tweaks and major additions.

The Basics of Modding & Preparing to Mod Minecraft

Before you go any further it's essential to note that modding the game can be both tricky and risky. Mojang won't be able to support you if you have problems with any mods and even experienced *Minecraft* communities may not be familiar with problems you may encounter. If you're unfamiliar with modding games the best approach to take is to be cautious, follow installation instructions carefully, and try out the game immediately after installing each mod to verify whether or not it has installed successfully – or broken something!

It's also worth noting that updates to *Minecraft* itself often break mods, although mod developers do generally try and keep up with the pace of change. For this reason, when downloading and installing a mod be sure to check which version(s) of the game it is compatible with.

Finally, it's worth backing up your existing worlds just in case. In Windows, you can access your game files by typing "appdata" into the Run command (press the Windows key then R), selecting Roaming, and selecting .minecraft. The saves folder contains your worlds. You can create an archive of the entire folder using the free utility WinRAR.

You'll also need to access the .minecraft folder in order to install mods – so you may wish to add it to your Favourites!

Mods like Mo'Creatures can add a sting to your tale.

Manually Installing Mods

There are two ways to install mods: manually, and using a launcher utility. This section covers the manual approach and the next the launcher approach.

Return to your .minecraft folder and open the folder called 'bin', in which you'll find a file called 'minecraft.jar'. That's an executable Java file, and it's the core of the game's data. You may also wish to back this up if you've previously installed any mods, though if you haven't there's not much point.

Open minecraft.jar with WinRAR: right-click on it, select 'Open With', and select 'WinRAR'. If WinRAR isn't in the list then select 'Choose default program' and locate WinRAR either in the displayed list or using the 'Browse' button to navigate to where it's installed. You should also de-select 'Always use the selected program to open this kind of file', especially if other people use the computer you're playing on.

Once your WinRAR window opens, you'll see a new list of folders and files with a variety of names. (Don't change anything unless instructions specify it – you could break the game!)

At this point, installing mods comes down to following the instructions provided by the mod's creator. It will usually involve adding something to minecraft.jar, deleting the folder called 'META-INF', and then closing the WinRAR window. However, do read the instructions provided with the mod files carefully, as not everything will be installed in the same way.

If something's gone wrong, don't despair! You can always delete your minecraft.jar file and launch your *Minecraft* .exe file – it should re-download the missing files automatically. If that doesn't work, delete the file called md5s alongside minecraft.jar and launch Minecraft.exe again.

If you find that an individual item in the game, or an item introduced by a mod, isn't functioning as it should, try to reinstall mods one at a time and try them out each in turn. Keep doing this until you find the broken item again. Now delete and replace your .jar file one more time, and install the last mod you installed before you install any others.

Try the game again: if the item is broken in the same way, you know that the mod has an issue with the game. If not, you know that it has an incompatibility with another mod. Install your other mods and try them out one at a time until you encounter the problem again.

Once you've narrowed down the problem in this way you can report it to the mod's author so that they can look at fixing it. In the meantime, you may have to avoid using a particular mod. Sadly, modding isn't a perfect world!

If the problem you're encountering is that the game launches to a black screen, the problem may be that the mod you've chosen is incompatible with the version of the game you're using. Double-check the installation guide and, in particular, which *Minecraft* versions the mod is compatible with. You can check your *Minecraft* version by launching the game and checking the version number in the bottom left of the main menu.

Using a Launcher to Install Mods

Another way to begin modding *Minecraft* is to acquire one or more launcher and modloader utilities. The two most popular launchers are Magic Launcher and MultiMC; opinions vary on which is best but one consensus is that MultiMC is more powerful whilst Magic Launcher is more friendly to newcomers. We're going to proceed with Magic Launcher, given that it's easier to get to grips with!

Once you've downloaded MagicLauncher you'll find that it can be immediately launched; you may want to store the file alongside your *Minecraft* executable and add a shortcut to your desktop. Once in Magic Launcher you'll see that the interface is familiar, bar a few tabs along the top (including Twitter feeds from Mojang's Notch and Jeb) and some new buttons along the bottom.

Clicking on the Setup button opens up the mod manager interface, and from here you can add, remove and otherwise manage installed mods. For now, however, it will be empty. You will see that you can change the 'Environment' drop-down to select a few different versions of *Minecraft* – either the latest version or older versions with which older mods will be compatible. This means you can play an older version with mods, but still try out the latest official updates without any mods – you just need to choose what you want to play today.

Another great feature of Magic Launcher is that it will try and tell you whether or not mods you've installed are compatible with the version of *Minecraft* you want to run, and you can even click 'Test' to see if the game launches successfully. This is a tremendously helpful way of installing mods easily! All you need to do is download the mods you want then click the 'Add' button, find them and select them.

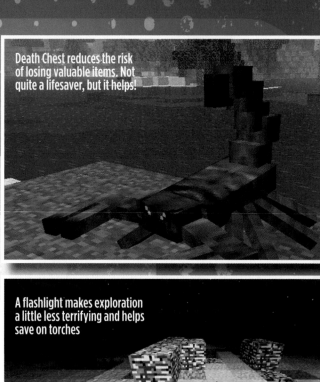

Death Chest reduces the risk of losing valuable items. Not quite a lifesaver, but it helps!

A flashlight makes exploration a little less terrifying and helps save on torches

Mods can change the way Minecraft generates new worlds, creating weird landscapes like this

Earthquakes are just one of the natural disasters mod users may add to their games. Insert joke about "dividing the community" here...

Some of our Favourite Mods

Whichever approach you take, you may want to install Modloader and/or Forge. These are APIs – essentially utilities that sit alongside *Minecraft*'s data files and help mods work alongside the core game successfully. They're often required by other mods, so getting them installed first off is a sensible plan. You may occasionally run into other pre-requisite installs like this, so again: read those installation instructions carefully. Now here's a list of mods to try out. You can find out more about them by searching the name online – check out the author's description and screenshots, the installation instructions, and install those that sound of interest to you!

As you get more and more interested in modding, you'll probably want to try new, different mods. Just as in Minecraft itself, modding is all about experimenting and exploring until you find out what you most enjoy. So don't be afraid to try something new!

Somewhere out there, there's the right mod for us all. We just have to find it

● **Optifine** – adds support for HD textures and provides a lot of options to improve visuals and game performance.

● **Mo'Creatures** – adds a host more critters including snails, elephants, komodo dragons all the way through to werewolves and ogres. Beware, some of the new creatures can destroy blocks!

● **Rei's Minimap** – adds a constantly-active minimap that helps map caves, place waypoints and spot nearby creatures.

● **Inventory Tweaks** – adds multiple minor alterations that make your life easier such as automatically replacing tools as they break and quick inventory/chest sorting.

● **Death Chest** – helps save items from destruction when you die. All you need to do is carry a chest around with you, and if you die the chest will be filled with as many items as it can carry.

● **The Flashlight** – helpful for exploring in the dark, though if you're attacked you'll have to choose between equipping a weapon and holding the torch!

● **Better World Generation** – gives you more customisation options when you create a new world.

● **Weather & Tornadoes** – for when a bit of rain just isn't enough! This mod adds wind, leaves and waves, plus extreme weather conditions.

● **Natural Disasters** – a good complement to Weather & Tornadoes, this adds earthquakes, meteors, volcanoes and sinkholes to the mix.

● **Treecapitator** – makes felling trees much easier. Chop out one block and down come the rest!

● **Single Player Commands** – if by 'mod' you mean 'cheat' or 'go crazy', this is for you.

● **TooManyItems** – an in-game inventory editor that will allow you to create unlimited stacks, save and load entire inventories, and create and enchant items on the fly. Again, this one looks a bit like cheating... a lot like cheating!

● **AMIDST** – this isn't actually a mod, but it's too useful not to mention. AMIDST is a separate utility you can install and open your *Minecraft* worlds with. It will then generate a top-down map of your world with biomes, villages, strongholds, witch huts and more displayed. Want to save time locating the closest Jungle biome? Use AMIDST.

10 ESSENTIAL TIPS FOR EXPERTS

1 Land With A Splash

If you're quick enough, you can use water to prevent yourself from dying in a fall. Select the bucket, look directly down and hammer the "place" button as you plummet. Time it correctly and you'll drop a water block on the ground just before you go splat. The water slows your descent instantly and painlessly, allowing you to survive an otherwise fatal plunge.

2 Fencing Tips

Fencing animals into a pen is useful when farming, but fences are just as good at keeping you out as they are at keeping animals in. The easiest way to get in and out of a pen is to replace one fencepost with a Netherbrick Fencepost. The two types of fence don't join up, allowing you to slip in and out, but the animals will be unable to follow you creating a handy, player-only filter.

3 Get Your Feet Wet

When mining Obsidian above a lava lake, there's always a chance of slipping in or having the Obsidian get incinerated by molten rock if you don't grab it quickly enough. To get around this problem, put a water block behind you and allow it to flow over your feet. It'll push you towards the lava, but the moment the Obsidian is mined the water will either create more or turn the flowing lava to cobblestone, ensuring your safety.

These chickens are idiots. You can walk straight out!

Trench foot is a preferable alternative to dying in a fire

4 Make Like a Frog

In *Minecraft* swimming is the least speedy way to get across water, but a boat-related mishap can leave you with no other option, right? Wrong! Lilypads can be placed on the surface of water. Swim to the surface, place one and get on top of it. Now, if you look down while jumping, you can place a new lilypad under your feet just before you land, keeping you out of the water and giving you a quicker way back to dry land.

5 Navigation Tips

Compasses are useful, but taking up a slot in your inventory means valuable space is wasted. Instead, you can navigate by looking at the sky. Clouds drift from south to north. Other blocks, such Redstone Dust and Cobblestone, have visible patterns that always face in the same direction. Learn them so you can navigate underground and you'll never need a compass again!

6 Create Blocks to carry more Stuff

The longer you play the game, the more crowded your inventory becomes. It's especially annoying if you want to transport a lot of material in one go. Luckily, resources such as metals, gems and minerals can be crafted into blocks on a crafting table (e.g. nine iron bars = one iron block). This means you can carry nine times as much resource in a single slot. Simply reverse the process when you reach your destination to recover the original items.

7 Slasher Moves

When fighting an enemy, they briefly change colour to indicate a hit has landed. While this is happening, they're invulnerable, but if you hammer the attack button your weapon will take damage even though it's having no effect. Expert players attack methodically, ensuring that every weapon lasts as long as it can.

8 Why Have Cotton?

The Silk Touch enchantment is not just useful for harvesting blocks for decoration – it's actually a massively useful tool for carrying increased resources. Consider that a block of glowstone shatters into between two and four piles of glowstone dust, meaning you can mine, at most, 32 blocks before an inventory slot is full, and in all probability much fewer. Mine glowstone blocks using Silk Touch, though, and you can carry 64 in one slot with ease!

9 All Eyes On Me

Ender Chests are a great item, allowing access to single storage spaces anywhere an Ender Chest is placed. But breaking an Ender Chest causes them to revert to Obsidian, lacking the Eye of Ender you need to rebuild a chest. You can try to get a pick with a Silk Touch enchantment to collect the chest without breaking it, but a simpler method is to keep a supply of Eyes of Ender in your Ender Chest.

10 One Final Tree-t

You can force saplings to grow larger by planting them in holes two blocks deep. This ensures that they turn into large trees rather than small ones, giving you more wood per sapling. Just make sure they get enough light!

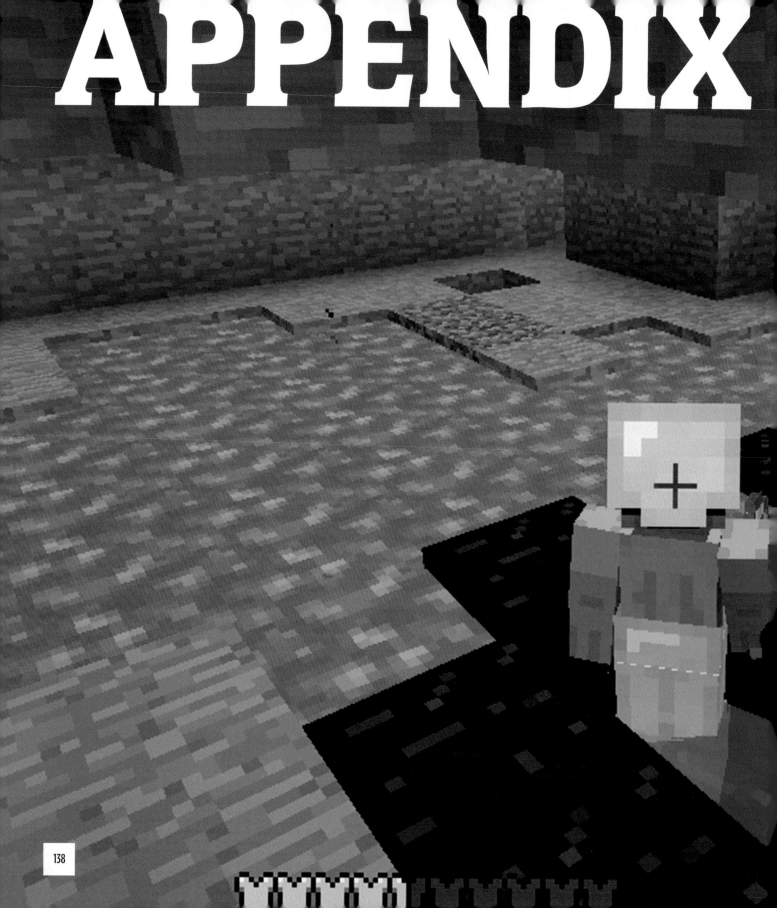

APPENDIX

Made it this far? Then hopefully by now you've picked up a whole host of new ideas, tactics, strategies and advice to help you get the most out of *Minecraft*! We're going to round the book off with a glossary for you to refer to as you play the game. And with that, we wish you well on your *Minecraft* adventures.

It's a great game, one we love a lot, and thank you for letting us share our love of it with you!

CRAFTING GLOSSARY

PLEASE NOTE: If you're hungry, and looking for food recipes, check the Minecraft Cookbook section of this guide.

BASIC ITEMS

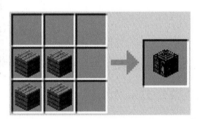

^ Crafting-Workbench

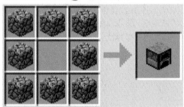

^ Crafting-Chest

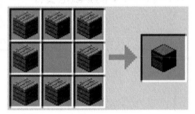

^ Crafting-Furnace

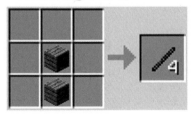

^ Crafting-Sticks

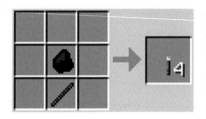

^ Crafting-Torches

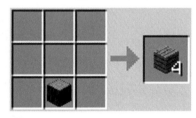

**^ Crafting-Planks1
Any wood block**

RESOURCE BLOCKS

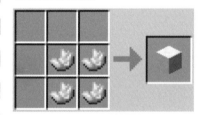

^ Block of quartz

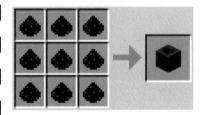

^ Block of fredstone

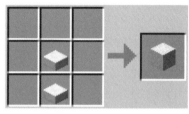

^ Chiseled quartz block

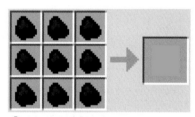

^ Coal block

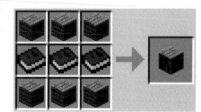

^ Crafting-Bookshelf

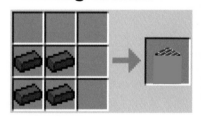

^ Crafting-Brickblock

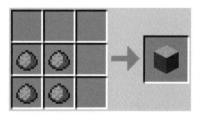

^ Crafting-Clayblock

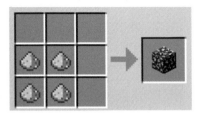

^ Crafting-Glowstone

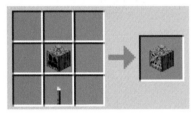

^ Crafting-Jack-O-Lantern1

^ Crafting-Ore-Blocks1
Iron, Gold, Diamond,
Lapis Lazuli, Emeralds,
Redstone, Coal

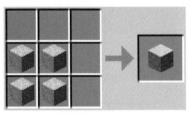

^ Crafting-Sandstone

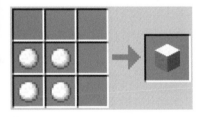

^ Crafting-Snowstone

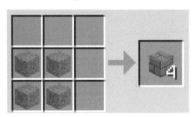

^ Crafting-Stonebrick

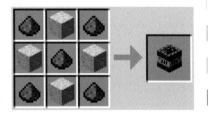

^ Crafting-TNT-Block

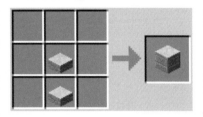

^ Decorative sandstone

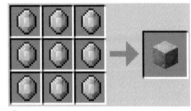

^ Emerald-Block

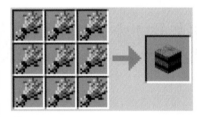

^ Haybale

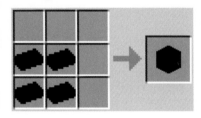

^ Netherbrick

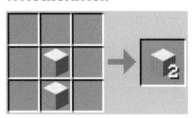

^ Pillar quartz block

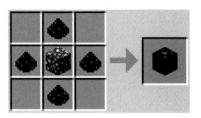

^ Red stone lamp

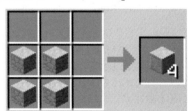

^ Smooth sandstone

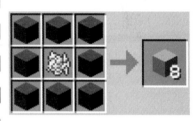

^ Stained clay
Any dye in the centre

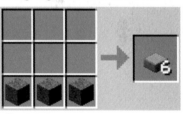

^ Stone slabs
Cobblestone, Brick,
Stone, Stone Brick or
Sandstone

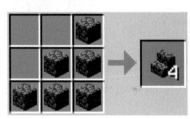

^ Stonestairs-updated
Cobblestone, Brick,
Nether Brick, Stone
Brick Quartz

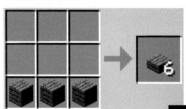

^ Wooden slabs
Any wooden planks

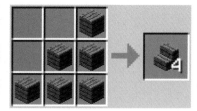

∧
∧ **Wooden stairs**

TOOLS

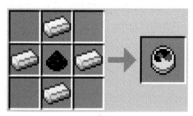

∧
∧ **Crafting axes**
**Wooden planks,
cobblestone, iron
ingots, gold ingots and
diamond**

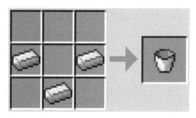

∧
∧ **Crafting bucket**

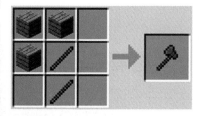

∧
∧ **Crafting watch**

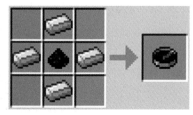

∧
∧ **Crafting compass**

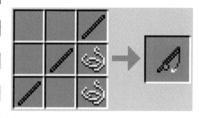

∧
∧ **Crafting fishing rod**

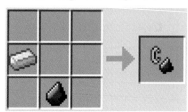

∧
∧ **Crafting flint and steel**

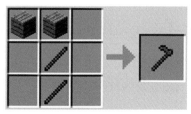

∧
∧ **Crafting Hoes**
**Wooden planks,
cobblestone, iron
ingots, gold ingots and
diamond**

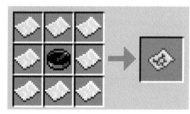

∧
∧ **Crafting map**

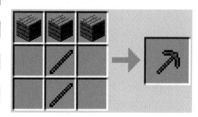

∧
∧ **Crafting Pickaxes1**
**Wooden planks,
cobblestone, iron ingots,
gold ingots and diamond**

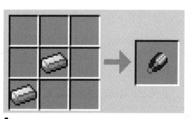

∧ **Crafting shears**

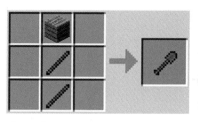

∧
∧ **Craftingshoevls**
**Wooden planks,
cobblestone, iron ingots,
gold ingots and diamond**

WEAPONS

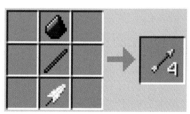

∧
∧ **Crafting arrows**

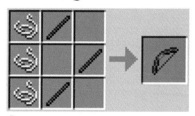

∧
∧ **Crafting bow**

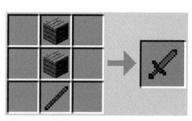

∧
∧ **Crafting swords**
**Wooden planks,
cobblestone, iron ingots,
gold ingots and diamond**

ARMOUR

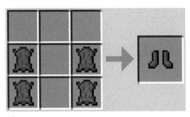

^ ^ **Crafting boots**
Leather, iron ingots, gold ingots, diamond

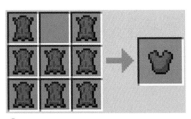

^ ^ **Crafting chestplates**
Leather, iron ingots, gold ingots, diamond

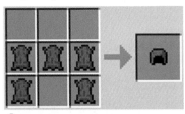

^ ^ **Crafting helmets**
Leather, iron ingots, gold ingots, diamond

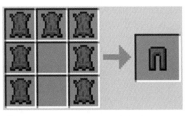

^ ^ **Crafting leggings**
Leather, iron ingots, gold ingots, diamond

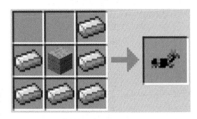

^ ^ **Horse armour**
Leather, iron ingots, gold ingots, diamond

MECHANISMS

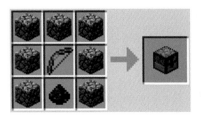

^ **Crafting dispenser**

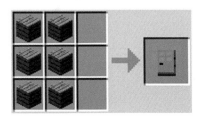

^ **Crafting doors**
Wooden planks or iron ingots

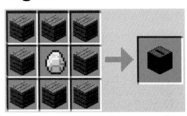

^ **Crafting jukebox**

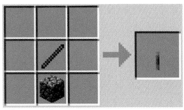

^ **Crafting lever**

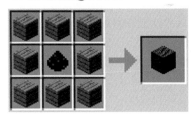

^ **Crafting notblock**

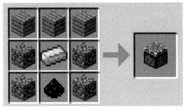

^ **Crafting piston**

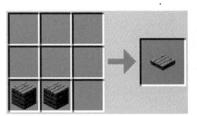

CRAFTING GLOSSARY

^ ^ **Crafting pressure plates1**
Wooden planks or stone blocks

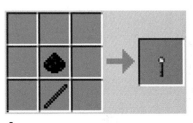

^ **Crafting red torch**

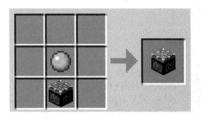

^ **Crafting sticky piston**

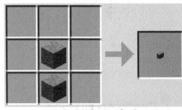

^ **Crafting stone button**

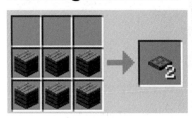

^ **Crafting trapdoor1**

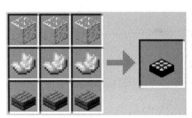

^ **Daylight sensor**

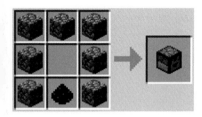

^
^ **Dropper**

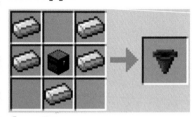

^
^ **Hopper**

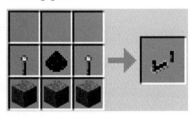

^
^ **Redstone repeater**

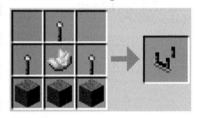

^
^ **Redstone comparator**

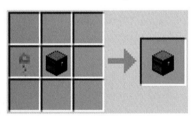

^
^ **Trapped chest**

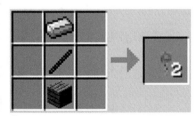

^
^ **Tripwire hook**

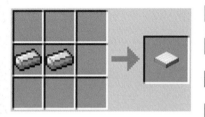

^
^ **Weight pressure plates
Iron ingots or gold
ingots**

TRANSPORT

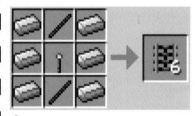

^
^ **Activatorrail**

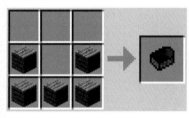

^
^ **Crafting Boat**

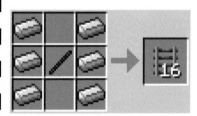

^
^ **Crafting Minecart-
Tracks**

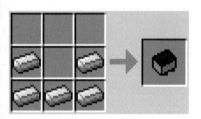

^
^ **Crafting Minecart**

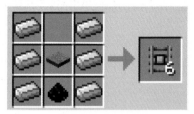

^
^ **Detector Rail**

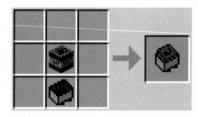

^
^ **Minecart with TNT**

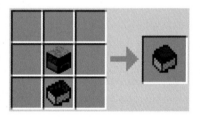

^
^ **Powered-Minecart-
Crafting**

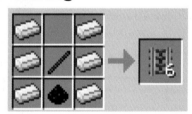

^
^ **Powered Rail**

ENCHANTMENT

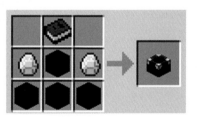

^
^ **Crafting-
Enchantment-Table**

BREWING

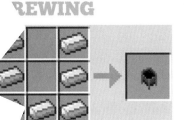

Cauldron

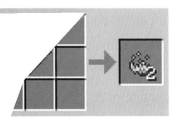

Crafting Blaze Powder

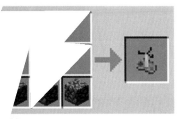

Crafting Brewing stand

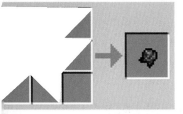

Crafting-Fermented-Spider-Eye

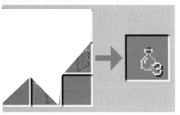

Crafting-Glass bottle

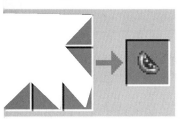

Crafting-Glistering-Melon

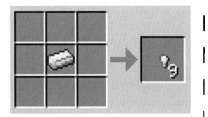

^ **Crafting Golden Nugget**

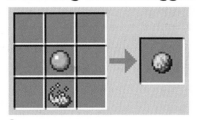

^ **Crafting Golden Nugget**

WOOL

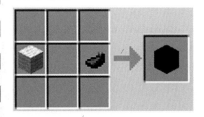

^ **Crafting-Black-Wool**

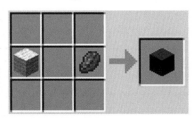

^ **Crafting-Blue-Wool**

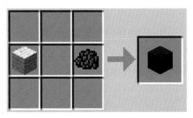

^ **Crafting-Brown-Wool**

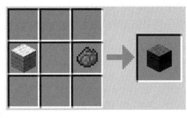

^ **Crafting-Cyan-Wool**

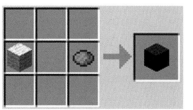

^ **Crafting-Gray-Wool**

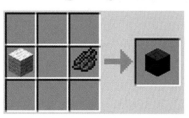

^ **Crafting-Green-Wool**

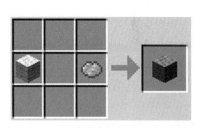

^ **Crafting-Light blue-Wool**

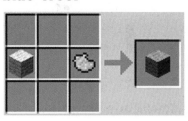

^ **Crafting-Light gray-Wool**

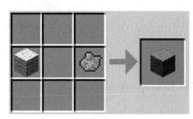

^ **Crafting-Orange-Wool**

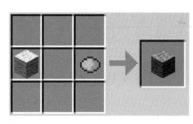

^ **Crafting-Pink-Wool**

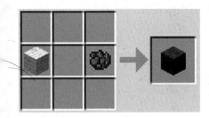

^ Crafting-Red-Wool

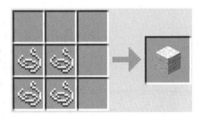

^ Crafting-Wool-Block

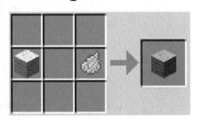

^ Crafting-Yellow-Wool

DYE

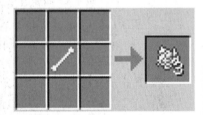

^ Crafting-Bone-Meal-White-Dye

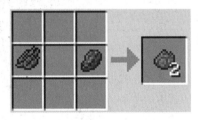

^ Crafting-Cyan-Dye1

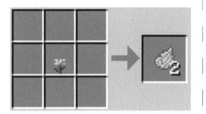

^ Crafting-Dandelion-Yellow

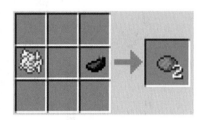

^ Crafting-Gray-Dye

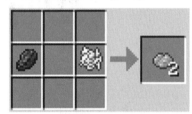

^ Crafting-Light-Blue-Dye

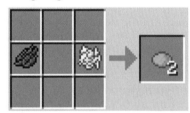

^ Crafting-Light-Gray-Dye

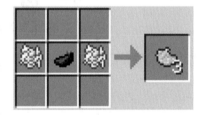

^ Crafting-Lime-Dye

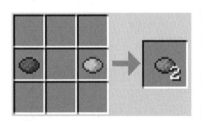

^ Crafting-Magenta-Dye

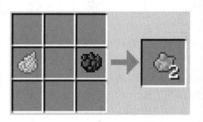

^ Crafting-Orange-Dye

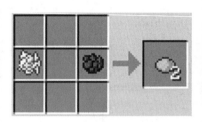

^ Crafting-Pink-Dye

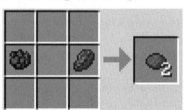

^ Crafting-Purple-Dye

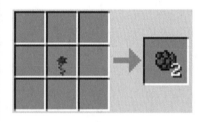

^ Crafting-Rose-Red

MISC

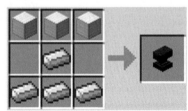

^ Anvil